Apress Pocket Guides

Apress Pocket Guides present concise summaries of cutting-edge developments and working practices throughout the tech industry. Shorter in length, books in this series aims to deliver quick-to-read guides that are easy to absorb, perfect for the time-poor professional.

This series covers the full spectrum of topics relevant to the modern industry, from security, AI, machine learning, cloud computing, web development, product design, to programming techniques and business topics too.

Typical topics might include:

- A concise guide to a particular topic, method, function or framework
- Professional best practices and industry trends
- A snapshot of a hot or emerging topic
- Industry case studies
- Concise presentations of core concepts suited for students and those interested in entering the tech industry
- Short reference guides outlining 'need-to-know' concepts and practices.

More information about this series at `https://link.springer.com/bookseries/17385`.

Practical PHP APIs with Symfony

A Step-by-Step Guide for Building Operation-Oriented APIs

Nacho Colomina Torregrosa

Apress®

Practical PHP APIs with Symfony: A Step-by-Step Guide for Building Operation-Oriented APIs

Nacho Colomina Torregrosa
Spain, Spain

ISBN-13 (pbk): 979-8-8688-2061-8   ISBN-13 (electronic): 979-8-8688-2062-5
https://doi.org/10.1007/979-8-8688-2062-5

Copyright © 2025 by Nacho Colomina Torregrosa

This work is subject to copyright. All rights are reserved by the Publisher, whether the whole or part of the material is concerned, specifically the rights of translation, reprinting, reuse of illustrations, recitation, broadcasting, reproduction on microfilms or in any other physical way, and transmission or information storage and retrieval, electronic adaptation, computer software, or by similar or dissimilar methodology now known or hereafter developed.

Trademarked names, logos, and images may appear in this book. Rather than use a trademark symbol with every occurrence of a trademarked name, logo, or image we use the names, logos, and images only in an editorial fashion and to the benefit of the trademark owner, with no intention of infringement of the trademark. The use in this publication of trade names, trademarks, service marks, and similar terms, even if they are not identified as such, is not to be taken as an expression of opinion as to whether or not they are subject to proprietary rights.

While the advice and information in this book are believed to be true and accurate at the date of publication, neither the authors nor the editors nor the publisher can accept any legal responsibility for any errors or omissions that may be made. The publisher makes no warranty, express or implied, with respect to the material contained herein.

> Managing Director, Apress Media LLC: Welmoed Spahr
> Acquisitions Editor: James Robinson-Prior
> Editorial Assistant: Gryffin Winkler

Cover designed by eStudioCalamar

Distributed to the book trade worldwide by Springer Science+Business Media New York, 1 New York Plaza, New York, NY 10004. Phone 1-800-SPRINGER, fax (201) 348-4505, e-mail orders-ny@springer-sbm.com, or visit www.springeronline.com. Apress Media, LLC is a Delaware LLC and the sole member (owner) is Springer Science + Business Media Finance Inc (SSBM Finance Inc). SSBM Finance Inc is a **Delaware** corporation.

For information on translations, please e-mail booktranslations@springernature.com; for reprint, paperback, or audio rights, please e-mail bookpermissions@springernature.com.

Apress titles may be purchased in bulk for academic, corporate, or promotional use. eBook versions and licenses are also available for most titles. For more information, reference our Print and eBook Bulk Sales web page at http://www.apress.com/bulk-sales.

Any source code or other supplementary material referenced by the author in this book is available to readers on GitHub. For more detailed information, please visit https://www.apress.com/gp/services/source-code.

If disposing of this product, please recycle the paper

Table of Contents

About the Author ....**xi**

About the Technical Reviewer ....**xiii**

Acknowledgments ....**xv**

Section 1. Preface..**xvii**

Section 2. CRUD API Endpoints and Operation-Oriented Endpoints...**xix**

Section 3. Prerequisites...**xxiii**

Chapter 1: Crafting Inputs, Outputs, and Operations **1**

   Section 1. Request Inputs and Outputs..2

      The Input Model...3

      The Output Model..3

      Operation Input Models...4

      Operation Output Models..6

      Conclusion...7

   Section 2. Building Operations...7

      The Operation Interface..8

      The Operation Metadata 9

      An Operation Class..9

      Array Outputs As Operation Results 11

      Conclusion...13

TABLE OF CONTENTS

Section 3. Collecting and Discovering Operations 13
The Operation Collection 14
The Operation Configurator 15
Discovering Operations 18
Handling NotFoundOperationException Errors 19
Conclusion 21

Section 4. Lazy Operations 21
The LazyOperation Interface 22
Marking an Operation As Lazy 23
Modifying the OperationCollectionConfigurator 24
Conclusion 25

Section 5. Validating Operations 25
The Validation Service 25
Validating Before Performing the Operation 28
Handling Deserializing and Validating Errors 29
Conclusion 31

Section 6. Connecting the Dots: Building an API Endpoint 31
Creating the Controller 31
Conclusion 39

Section 7. Versioning the API 40
A New Metadata Parameter 40
Receiving the Version 40
Checking the Version 41
Checking for an OperationDoesNotSupportApiVersionException in the KernelSubscriber 43
Conclusion 43

Section 8. Monitoring Operations 44
Creating a Monolog Handler 44
Creating a Logging Wrapper to Log Operations Execution Information 45

TABLE OF CONTENTS

Writing to the Log When an Operation Request Is Received 48
Writing to the Log When an Operation Request Ends 50
Conclusion 54

Chapter 2: Securing Operations **55**

Section 1. The User 55
The User Entity 55
Loading the Database with Users 59
Conclusion 60
Section 2. Protecting the Endpoint 61
The Operation Authenticator 61
The Firewall and the User Provider 64
Conclusion 65
Section 3. Protecting the Operations 65
The Abstract Operation Voter 66
The Operation Voter 67
Handling Access Denied Errors 70
Checking for Permission 72
Conclusion 73
Section 4. Accessing the Logged User from Operations 74
The OperationRequiresUserInterface 74
Passing the User to the Operation 74
Implementing the OperationRequiresUserInterface 76
Conclusion 77
Section 5. Validating Operations According to the User Role 77
Using Validation Groups in the Input Model 77
Specifying That the Operation Uses Groups 79
Adapting the Validation Handler to Use Groups 80

vii

TABLE OF CONTENTS

Adapting the ApiOperationHandler to Pass the Groups 81
Conclusion 82
Section 6. Controlling Requests 83
The Token-Bucket Strategy 83
Configuring Token-Bucket Strategy 84
Using the Limiter 84
Conclusion 87

Chapter 3: Background Execution of API Operations 89

Section 1. Marking Operations As Background..90
Conclusion 91
Section 2. The Operation Message and Handler 92
Creating the Operation Message 92
Creating the Operation Handler 93
Conclusion 94
Section 3. Sending Operations to the Background 94
Conclusion 98
Section 4. Routing Operations 98
Consuming Messages 99
Managing Workers..100
Checking the Transport Works 101
Retrying Failed Operations 104
Conclusion 105
Section 5. Prioritizing Operations..105
Defining the Priorities 106
Modifying the Metadata Attribute 106
Creating a Message for the HIGH Priority Operations................................107
Creating a Transport for Each Priority...107
Modifying the Message Handler 108

TABLE OF CONTENTS

    Dispatching the Message Depending on the Priority 110

    Conclusion 111

  Section 6. Triggering Post-Execution Notifications 111

    Marking an Operation to Send a Notification 112

    Creating the Event and the Subscriber 112

    Creating the Notifier Service 114

    Handling the Notification Based on the Operation 115

    Using the Notifier Service 118

    Triggering the Event 119

    Conclusion 120

Chapter 4: Context-Specific Operations 121

  Section 1. Contextualizing an Endpoint 122

    The Context Enumeration 122

    The OperationContext Attribute 123

    Wrapping an Endpoint with a Context 124

    Conclusion 125

  Section 2. Detecting Endpoints in a Context Specified 126

    Listening to the Kernel Controller Event 126

    Conclusion 129

Chapter 5: Testing the API 131

  Section 1. Creating the Test Class 131

    Conclusion 132

  Section 2. The API Tests 133

    Test a Successful Operation Execution 133

    Test a Successful Background Operation 134

    Test Invalid Operation Data 135

    Test an Unexisting Operation 136

    Test Missing Operation 137

TABLE OF CONTENTS

Test an Invalid User Token 138
Testing Unauthorized User 138
Testing an Invalid Context 139
Making a Short Refactory 140
Executing the Tests 141
Conclusion 141

Afterword..143

About the Author

Nacho Colomina Torregrosa has been working as a PHP developer for the last 12 years, in which he has largely focused on the utilization of the Symfony framework. During this time, he has had the opportunity to observe the growth of PHP and Symfony and feels very fortunate to have participated in very interesting projects with a team made up of wonderful people.

He is passionate about the blockchain sector and how Web3 and decentralized applications can change many industries, not just finance. He is self-learning how to program smart contracts and how to apply them in various sectors such as finance, real estate, and even democratic participation. Nacho has participated in several hackathons organized by the Stellar Foundation, where he had to create a contract/application and deploy it on the Soroban platform. This has provided Nacho with knowledge about the blockchain ecosystem, and he had the opportunity to see the work of other fantastic developers.

He is passionate about the open source movement and tries to contribute to the wider open source community and projects as much as possible. As a result, Nacho developed Equillar, a PHP/Symfony-based open-source fintech platform powered by Soroban smart-contracts, offering a ready-to-use technical foundation for organizations to build upon `https://equillar.com`.

About the Technical Reviewer

Vadim Atamanenko is an experienced software engineer and technical reviewer with over 25 years of expertise in software development. His professional journey includes a leadership role in the analytical reporting department of the major holding company, Freedom Holding Corp. Throughout his career, he has actively contributed to the scientific community, publishing articles on the application of artificial intelligence in the financial sector.

His technical expertise has been internationally recognized, evidenced by his membership in two prestigious associations: IEEE (Institute of Electrical and Electronics Engineers) and Leaders Excellence at Harvard Square. His scientific papers have been published in various scholarly journals, including *Modern Science: Current Issues in Theory and Practice*.

As a technical reviewer, he also has experience reviewing technical literature. His review of a technical book combines in-depth technical understanding with practical experience in software development. He is eager to share his knowledge and insights with readers, shedding light on important topics and innovations in the world of technology.

Acknowledgments

My heartfelt thanks to the open source community, and especially to the Symfony community. Your dedication, collaboration, and commitment to free software have been an inspiration and an indispensable foundation for this book.

Section 1. Preface

In this book, we will learn to construct a robust and efficient API architecture that revolves around operations. By the end of this, you will have the knowledge and necessary skills to build an operation-oriented API using the PHP programming language and the Symfony framework.

This book is designed to provide you with a comprehensive understanding of how to create a single API endpoint that embraces the concept of operations. We will utilize the robust features of Symfony to build an environment where operations are the focal point of our API design.

Please note that this book assumes a certain level of familiarity with the Symfony framework. It is not intended to serve as a comprehensive guide of Symfony but rather as a focused exploration of its powerful features for building an operation-oriented API.

It's also important to clarify that this book does not delve into the development of specific operations themselves. While we may use operation examples like "SendPayment" for illustrative purposes, the primary goal is to demonstrate how to construct the necessary code to discover, manage, and execute operations.

Throughout the chapters, we will cover essential Symfony topics such as dependency injection features, security authentication, and background operations with Symfony Messenger.

Section 2. CRUD API Endpoints and Operation-Oriented Endpoints

CRUD-Based API Endpoints

Developers usually build APIs using the REST approach, that is, focusing on resources. To expose the operations that clients can perform over those resources, we usually follow the CRUD acronym, which means **CREATE**, **READ**, **UPDATE**, and **DELETE**. Each word represents an operation, so it means that for each resource we can

- Create a new element
- Read from the resource listing the current elements
- Update an existing element
- Remove an existing element

When we refer to a resource, we can think about a collection of elements (for instance, a book resource).

When defining the resource API calls, we normally set up an HTTP endpoint for each CRUD operation we want to expose. Let's see an example for a book resource:

- **GET** /api/v1/book
- **GET** /api/v1/book/{id}

SECTION 2. CRUD API ENDPOINTS AND OPERATION-ORIENTED ENDPOINTS

- **POST** /api/v1/book
- **PATCH** /api/v1/book/{id}
- **DELETE** /api/v1/book/{id}

As you can see above

- The **GET** endpoints perform the **READ** operations.
- The **POST** endpoint performs the **CREATE** operation.
- The **PATCH** endpoint performs the **UPDATE** operation.
- The **DELETE** endpoint performs the **DELETE** operation.

This approach covers basic operations. What happens when we want to expose more complex operations? Let's explore it in the next section.

Operation-Oriented Endpoints

Imagine an e-commerce API with an endpoint for orders (*api/v1/orders/{orderId}*) where we want to approve an order placed by a customer. With a simple PATCH request, you might send a payload like this:

```
PATCH api/v1/orders/{orderId}
{
 "status": "approved"
}
```

This approach works, but it doesn't explicitly convey the intent behind the update. The server needs to understand that "approved" refers to approving the order, not just changing a generic "status" field. Approving an order may involve more tasks than just updating the value of the status field.

SECTION 2. CRUD API ENDPOINTS AND OPERATION-ORIENTED ENDPOINTS

Let's consider the operation we want to execute as a resource. To do it, we would create an order operation resource that would receive the operation to perform and the data required to perform this operation:

POST /api/v1/orders/operation
```
{
 "operation" : "ApproveOrder",
 "data" : {
 "id" : 1559877444
 }
}
```

This is a clearer approach since the payload operation name explicitly communicates the purpose of the request. It helps us to go one step further and specify business actions through an operation endpoint. However, this approach could complicate the generation of API documentation since we only have a single endpoint. Let's consider the following alternatives:

POST /api/v1/operation/approve-order
```
{
    "id" : 1559877444
}
```
PATCH /api/v1/orders/:id/approve-order

The above alternatives would facilitate the creation of documentation, and at the same time, our API would continue to focus on the operation.

We will see during the last section of Chapter 1 that we can define our endpoints in other ways while keeping our API operationally oriented. The way to discover, retrieve, and execute operations will be the same regardless of how we define our endpoints.

This approach requires discovering the operation to be executed, obtaining the associated handler, and executing the operation using the data received. We will learn how to code it using PHP and the Symfony framework during the course of the book.

SECTION 2. CRUD API ENDPOINTS AND OPERATION-ORIENTED ENDPOINTS

Conclusion

In this section, we have exposed the advantages we can take when using an operation-oriented approach to build our API. The next section will give us a brief guide about what Symfony components and backend services we are going to use before starting to write code.

Section 3. Prerequisites

This section offers a concise overview of the Symfony components and backend services that will be utilized in the upcoming chapters, along with instructions for their installation.

The code of this book has been written using the PHP 8.3 version and the Symfony version 7.3.

Symfony Components

Symfony Serializer Pack

The Symfony Serializer Component provides a simple and efficient way to serialize and deserialize data. It allows us to convert PHP data structures, such as arrays and objects, into a format that can be easily stored or transmitted, such as JSON or XML. In the same way, this component also allows us to deserialize raw data (JSON, XML) into PHP classes. We will need this component to deserialize API inputs and serialize API outputs.

Symfony Validator

The Symfony Validator component provides a way to validate data. It allows you to define rules and constraints for your data and then checks if the data conforms to those rules. The component provides a wide range of built-in validators, such as checks for email addresses, URLs, and credit card numbers, as well as more complex validation logic.

We will need this component to validate the required data to execute an operation so that we can avoid errors during the execution.

SECTION 3. PREREQUISITES

Symfony Security

The Symfony Security Component provides a set of tools for handling authentication, authorization, and other security-related tasks in Symfony applications. With features such as user authentication, access control, and firewall configuration, the Security Component helps developers implement robust security measures to protect their applications from unauthorized access and potential security threats.

We will use this component in Chapter 2 to create a firewall to protect our API endpoint and we will also use voters to authorize operations to certain users based, for instance, on their roles.

Symfony Messenger

The Symfony Messenger Component simplifies the process of sending and receiving messages within Symfony applications. It enables developers to decouple application logic by using message buses, handlers, and transports to handle message processing asynchronously. By leveraging the Messenger Component, developers can streamline communication between different parts of their application, improving scalability and maintainability.

We will use this component in Chapter 3 to execute operations in the background. Furthermore, we also need to install the corresponding messenger transport package depending on which we are going to use. In this book, we are using Redis as a routing transport, so we will need to install the redis-messenger package too. We will also need to install the doctrine-messenger component since we will route the failed operations to a doctrine transport.

Symfony ORM Pack

The Symfony Doctrine Component is a powerful tool that integrates the Doctrine ORM (Object-Relational Mapping) library into Symfony applications. This component simplifies database interactions by mapping database tables to PHP objects, allowing developers to work with database records as if they were regular PHP objects. With features such as entity mapping, query building, and database migrations, the Symfony Doctrine Component provides a robust and efficient way to manage database operations within Symfony applications.

We need this component since we are going to create a **User** entity in Chapter 2 to store the users who will be able to access our API. We will also need it in Chapter 3 because we will route failed operations to a doctrine transport.

Symfony Doctrine Fixtures Bundle

The Symfony Doctrine Fixtures Bundle is a tool that allows developers to easily manage and load sample data into a Symfony application's database. It provides a way to create and execute data fixtures, which are Symfony services that define the sample data to be loaded into the database. We need these services to load users to our **User** entity.

Symfony String

The Symfony String component provides a set of useful classes and functions for working with strings in PHP. The component includes classes for manipulating strings, such as trimming, padding, and splitting, as well as classes for working with URLs, inflectors, and slugifiers.

SECTION 3. PREREQUISITES

We will use this component in the last section of Chapter 1 to camelize an operation name.

Symfony Maker Bundle

The Symfony Maker Bundle is a developer-friendly tool that automates the creation of common Symfony elements, such as controllers, entities, forms, and more. We will use this component to generate the **User** entity and to generate the API tests in the last chapter.

Symfony Rate Limiter

The Symfony Rate Limiter component allows developers to control the rate of requests made to an application. It helps prevent abuse by limiting the number of requests a user can make within a specific time frame. This component provides a flexible and customizable way to implement rate-limiting strategies, such as frame window and token bucket, to ensure system stability and security.

To install this component, we will have to install the Symfony Lock component too.

Symfony Test-Pack

The Symfony Test Pack is a component that integrates the PhpUnit test tool and provides a set of tools and utilities to help you write and run tests for your Symfony-based applications. It includes a range of features such as a test client, a profiler, and a set of assertions to make testing easier and more efficient. We will need this component so that we can write the API tests in the last chapter.

SECTION 3. PREREQUISITES

Installing Composer

Before creating the Symfony project, we must install Composer. Composer is the most commonly used PHP package manager, and it is required to create the project and to install the Symfony components. To download and install it, refer to the official docs.

Creating the Symfony Project

We will need to install the **symfony-cli** tool to create a new Symfony project. Follow the official download Symfony docs to install it. After installing, we are ready to create the project. To do it, we must execute the following command within a folder of your choice.

```
symfony new <your_project_name> --version="7.3.*"
```

The above command should create the basic folder structure and install the framework-required libraries.

Installing the Components

After having the project created, we have to install the components we have talked about in the previous sections. To install it, you must use composer:

```
composer require symfony/messenger
composer require symfony/redis-messenger
composer require symfony/doctrine-messenger
composer require symfony/orm-pack
composer require symfony/security-bundle
composer require --dev symfony/maker-bundle
composer require --dev orm-fixtures
```

SECTION 3. PREREQUISITES

```
composer require symfony/lock
composer require symfony/rate-limiter
composer require symfony/string
composer require --dev symfony/test-pack
```

After installing the test component, ensure PhpUnit has been installed by running the following command: *bin/phpunit* from the project root folder.

Installing the Database

As we will create a User entity in Chapter 2, we will need to have a ready-to-use database. We are using SQLite to manage our database. To install it, we are going to use docker and docker-compose.

Feel free to use the database you want (MySOL, Postgres, MariaDB ...) and to install it using the procedure you consider appropriate. Personally, I like using docker since it's easy to create new containers without having to install services on my computer, and there are plenty of pre-built images available in the docker hub.

Let's create the *docker-compose.yaml* file in our project root folder and add the SQLite service:

```yaml
version: '3'

services:
  sqlite3:
    image: keinos/sqlite3:latest
    volumes:
      - './db:/var/db'
```

As you can see, we are going to use the latest SQlite3 image version (you can use any other image of your choice) and we are creating a new volume that links the container *db* folder with our *var/db* folder. To start the container, use the following command:

```
docker compose up -d
```

Then, we only have to add the **DATABASE_URL** environment variable to the *.env* file, which is located in the project root folder.

```
DATABASE_URL="sqlite:///%kernel.project_dir%/var/db/data.db"
```

This variable contains the path to the SQLite database file. This path matches with the volume path defined in the compose file. Ensure you have created the directory var/db.

Installing Redis

Redis is an open source, in-memory database that can be used as a cache or message broker among other uses. It supports various data structures such as strings, hashes, lists, sets, and streams. It is known for its high performance and versatility in handling data. We are going to use Redis as a messenger transport in Chapter 3. As we did with SQLite, we are going to install it using docker.

As I said before, feel free to install redis following a procedure of your choice.

Let's add the Redis service to our compose file.

```
version: '3'

services:
  sqlite3:
    image: sqlite:latest
    volumes:
      - './db:/var/db'
```

SECTION 3. PREREQUISITES

```
redis:
  image: redis
  ports:
    - '6401:6379'
```

As you can see, we are using the Redis image and linking the container Redis port 6379 to our computer port 6401. Let's start the Redis container by executing the compose up command again:

```
docker compose up -d
```

This will create the container for the recently added Redis service. Now, as we did before with the **DATABASE_URL** environment variable, let's add the **MESSENGER_TRANSPORT_DSN** variable which will contain the redis dsn where the messages will be routed.

```
MESSENGER_TRANSPORT_DSN=redis://localhost:6401/operations
```

The operations path indicates the Redis stream name where the messages will be queued.

The redis-messenger component uses redis streams to queue messages. You can learn more about them by following the last link, but you must not worry about how they work since the symfony messenger does all the routing work internally.

Conclusion

This section has helped us to know and install all the necessary components and backend services that we will need throughout the entire book. Now, we can start to write some code in the first chapter, where we will build the basic skeleton of an operation-oriented API.

CHAPTER 1

Crafting Inputs, Outputs, and Operations

In this chapter, we are going to build the basic core functionalities of an operation-oriented API. Specifically, we will write the necessary code to

- Create models to represent inputs and outputs
- Create services to represent operations
- Create an accessible collection to store and retrieve those operations
- Perform operations based on the request payload
- Validate payloads
- Create the endpoint to receive and perform the operation requests

CHAPTER 1   CRAFTING INPUTS, OUTPUTS, AND OPERATIONS

Section 1. Request Inputs and Outputs

In the context of an API request, the following is a quick breakdown of inputs and outputs:

- **Inputs**: This refers to the data or instructions you provide to the API. These typically come in the request payload or headers, depending on the API design. For instance, in a "send payment" operation, the inputs might include the recipient's information, the amount, and potentially a reference code.

- **Outputs**: This is the data or response you receive back from the API after it processes your request. The output format can vary depending on the API, but it often comes in JSON or XML format. For example, the output for a "send payment" operation might be a confirmation message with a success status and a transaction ID.

In the next sections, we are going to create a class for both the request input and output so that we can deserialize and validate them later.

> You will notice in this section that some models' properties are wrapped with some Symfony validation constraints. In "Section 5. Validating Operations," we will learn how to validate those models according to the constraints that their properties hold.

The Input Model

Below we can find a class that represents an API input request model.

```
namespace App\Api\Input;
use Symfony\Component\Validator\Constraints\NotBlank;

readonly class ApiInput
{
    public function __construct(
        #[NotBlank(message: 'Operation name cannot be empty')]
        public string $operation,
        public array $data = []
    ){}
}
```

The input model contains the following properties:

- **Operation**: Holds the name of the operation we want to execute.
- **Data**: Holds the data that the operation requires to be performed. If the operation requires no data, then this property can be empty.

The previous **ApiInput** model uses the NotBlank Symfony validation constraint, which means that the operation name cannot be empty.

The Output Model

```
namespace App\Api\Output;

readonly class ApiOutput
{
    public function __construct(
        public mixed $data,
```

```
    public int $code
){ }
}
```

The output model contains the following properties:

- **Data**: The operation execution result. It could be an object array, a simple object, or even be empty if the operation returns no result.

- **Code**: The HTTP code returned within the response. We should take into account the following tips to choose the output HTTP code:

    - If we return the final operation result, we should opt for a 200 OK HTTP code.

    - If we return an operation process tracking key (the endpoint accepts the execution, but it's been delayed), we should opt for a 202 ACCEPTED HTTP code.

    - If we do not return any operation result, we should opt for a 204 NO CONTENT HTTP code. 204 should only be used when no content is returned at all, not even an empty JSON object.

Operation Input Models

Each operation might require some data for execution. For instance, a payment operation should require the amount to pay and the payment receiver. Each operation input model will be different from each other since each operation performs a different task.

CHAPTER 1 CRAFTING INPUTS, OUTPUTS, AND OPERATIONS

The following example shows a hypothetical model for a payment operation:

```php
use Symfony\Component\Validator\Constraints as Assert;

readonly class SendPaymentInput
{
    public function __construct(
        #[Assert\NotBlank(message: 'Receiver cannot be empty')]
        public string $receiver,
        #[Assert\NotBlank(message: 'Amount cannot be empty')]
        #[Assert\GreaterThan(0, message: 'Amount must be greater than 0')]
        public float|int $amount,
    ){}
}
```

As the previous ApiInput model, the *SendPaymentInput* model also uses the NotBlank symfony constraint to specify that both sender and amount properties values are required. It means that a *SendPayment* operation cannot be performed if any of these values are missing. Furthermore, it uses the GreaterThan constraint to specify that the amount must be greater than 0.

The last input specifies that both receiver and amount properties are required. However, there may be input models where certain parameters can be optional. For instance, the **SendPaymentInput** model could include an optional payment label. We can utilize PHP type hinting to designate the label as optional:

```php
use Symfony\Component\Validator\Constraints as Assert;

readonly class SendPaymentInput
{
```

5

CHAPTER 1   CRAFTING INPUTS, OUTPUTS, AND OPERATIONS

```
    public function __construct(
        #[Assert\NotBlank(message: 'Receiver cannot be empty')]
        public string $receiver,
        #[Assert\NotBlank(message: 'Amount cannot be empty')]
        #[Assert\GreaterThan(0, message: 'Amount must be
        greater than 0')]
        public float|int $amount,
        public ?string $label = null
    ){}
}
```

As you can see, the model declares the label as an optional string (using the "?" modifier) and assigns *null* as a default value.

Operation Output Models

In the same way that we create models for the input data, we can create models to represent the output data. Continuing with the example of the SendPaymentInput operation, let's create an output model that would hold two properties: *id* and *status*.

```
readonly class SendPaymentOutput
{
    public function __construct(
        public string $id,
        public string $status
    ){}
}
```

This output model would be used after performing an operation to represent the result.

```
$id = '......';
$status = 'ACCEPTED';
```

```
return new ApiOutput(
    new SendPaymentOutput($id, $status),
    202
);
```

This way is better than using raw arrays because it provides a clear structure for the data being returned. This makes it easier for developers to understand the expected response format.

For operations which return result data from the database (for instance, an operation that returns a list of elements for a Client entity), we should create concrete output data objects instead of directly serializing the entities. By creating specific output objects (also known as DTOs – Data Transfer Objects), you maintain a clear separation between business logic and data representation. This helps prevent persistence logic and infrastructure concerns from leaking into the presentation layer.

In the next section, we will analyze a complete example.

Conclusion

In this section, we've created the basic models we will need to start building operations. In the next section, we will learn how to create operations and how to create the necessary services to hold them.

Section 2. Building Operations

This section outlines the key principles for creating well-defined API operations:

- **Interface Enforcement**: Every operation must implement a specific interface. This interface defines a standard method that all operations must use to encapsulate their execution logic. This promotes consistency and simplifies operation management.

- **Metadata for Clarity**: Each operation will be marked with a metadata attribute. This attribute serves as a central location to store essential information about the operation, such as its name and the class representing its input model. This metadata enhances code readability and simplifies operation discovery.

In summary, these principles ensure well-structured and maintainable API operations with clear execution logic and readily accessible metadata.

The Operation Interface

The **OperationInterface** acts as a contract that all operations must implement. The **perform** method will be the one that the operations will use to encapsulate its logic.

```
namespace App\Api\Operation;

use App\Api\Output\ApiOutput;
use Symfony\Component\DependencyInjection\Attribute\
Autoconfigure;

#[Autoconfigure(tags: ['api.operation'])]
interface OperationInterface
{
    public function perform(mixed $data): ApiOutput;
}
```

The AutoConfigure attribute tells the Symfony kernel to tag as "api.operation" those services which implement this interface. This means that each operation will be tagged as such after implementing the **OperationInterface**.

The **perform** method must return an instance of the ApiOutput class. If you remember from the last section, this class holds the operation request result.

The Operation Metadata

The operation metadata attribute holds two properties. The first one specifies the operation name, and the second one specifies the operation input model class.

```
namespace App\Api\Attribute;

#[\Attribute(\Attribute::TARGET_CLASS)]
readonly class OperationMetadata
{
    public function __construct(
      public string $name,
      public ?string $input = null
    ){ }
}
```

A request operation payload will be deserialized to the input class, specified with the "$input" parameter, before executing the operation. If the input class properties are annotated with Symfony validation constraints, the deserialized model will also be validated to ensure that the received data is valid.

We will see this entire process during the rest of the chapter.

An Operation Class

So far, we know that an operation must implement the OperationInterface and has to be flagged with the OperationMetadata attribute. In this section, we are showing an example of an operation class.

CHAPTER 1   CRAFTING INPUTS, OUTPUTS, AND OPERATIONS

```php
namespace App\Api\Operation;

use App\Api\Attribute\OperationMetadata;
use App\Api\Input\Operation\SendPaymentInput;
use App\Api\Output\ApiOutput;

#[OperationMetadata(
 name: 'SendPayment',
 input: SendPaymentInput::class
)]
class SendPaymentOperation implements OperationInterface
{
    /**
     * @param SendPaymentInput $data
     */
    public function perform(mixed $data): ApiOutput
    {
            // This method would hold the code in charge of
            sending the payment
        $id = '......';
        $status = 'ACCEPTED';

            return new ApiOutput(new SendPaymentOutput($id,
            $status), 202);
    }
}
```

The operation metadata attribute specifies the operation name (**SendPayment**) and the input data class name (SendPaymentInput). The **perform** method would execute the operation and return the **ApiOutput** containing the result as an output model and the HTTP response code.

CHAPTER 1   CRAFTING INPUTS, OUTPUTS, AND OPERATIONS

To prevent hardcoding the operation name in the metadata name parameter, we can create a PHP enumeration where to centralize all the operation names:

```
enum OperationNames
{
    case SendPayment;
}
```

Now, we can change the OperationMetadata name parameter with this:

```
#[OperationMetadata(
    name: OperationNames::SendPayment->name,
    input: SendPaymentInput::class
)]
```

Array Outputs As Operation Results

In the previous section, we talked about operations that return the result data from the database. We specified that it would be better to create a concrete output instead of directly serializing database entities so that we can prevent persistence logic and infrastructure concerns from leaking into the presentation layer. Let's imagine we are creating an operation to return the clients' data stored in our database. We could name that operation: **GetClients**.

Before creating the operation, we are going to create an output model for the client entity. Let's imagine that we only want to return the name, the corporate email, the contact's name, and contact phone.

```
readonly class ClientOutput {
    public function __construct(
        public string $name,
        public string $email,
```

11

CHAPTER 1   CRAFTING INPUTS, OUTPUTS, AND OPERATIONS

```php
        public string $contactName,
        public string $contactPhone
    ){}
}
```

Now, we are ready to create the **GetClientsOperation** class

```php
#[OperationMetadata(
    name: 'GetClients',
    input: GetClientsInput::class
)]
class GetClientsOperation implements OperationInterface
{
    public function __construct(
        private readonly EntityManagerInterface $em
    ){}

    /**
     * @param GetClientsInput $data
     */
    public function perform(mixed $data): ApiOutput
    {
        $clients = $this->em->getRepository(Client::class)->findAll();
        $clientsOutput = [];

        foreach($clients as $client) {
            $clientsOutput[] = new ClientOutput(
                $client->getName(),
                $client->getEmail(),
                $client->getContactName(),
```

```
            $client->getContactPhone()
        );
    }

    return new ApiOutput($clientsOutput, 200);
    }
}
```

As you can see in the code above, if changes are made to the Client entity, it will not affect the presentation layer, which will prevent certain types of errors, such as circular references during serialization.

I would like to emphasize that the code responsible for looping through the clients and creating a ClientOutput for each one should be placed outside of the main operation, ideally in a separate service. By doing this, we can effectively decouple the functionality, enhancing maintainability and scalability. Since this is not a book about SOLID principles or how to create domain-oriented applications, we will not go into further detail on this aspect.

Conclusion

We have established the core elements of the operation-oriented APIs: operations and their associated metadata. In the next section, we'll explore how to effectively discover and collect these defined operations, ensuring they are readily accessible within our API.

Section 3. Collecting and Discovering Operations

We've established how to create individual API operations using the OperationInterface and the OperationMetadata attribute. Now, let's explore how to build a service specifically designed to manage these operations. This service will

- **Hold a Collection of Operations**: The service will act as a central repository, storing all the defined operations within your application.

- **Retrieve Operations by Name**: We will be able to efficiently retrieve a specific operation by its unique name within the service. This simplifies operation lookup and promotes code clarity.

By creating this service, we will achieve a more organized and efficient way to manage and access API operations within the application.

The Operation Collection

First, we need to create a class for storing the operations collection.

```php
namespace App\Api\Collection;

class OperationCollection
{
    private array $operations;

    public function setOperations(array $operations): void
    {
        $this->operations = $operations;
    }

    public function getOperation(string $operation): ApiOperation
    {
        if(!isset($this->operations[$operation])){
```

CHAPTER 1   CRAFTING INPUTS, OUTPUTS, AND OPERATIONS

```
            throw new NotFoundOperationException(sprintf('Operation
            %s is not defined', $operation));
    }

        return $this->operations[$operation];
    }
}
```

The operation collection is straightforward. It simply contains a setter to load the operations and a getter to get a concrete operation. If an operation does not exist, it throws a **NotFoundOperationException**.

We will create this exception later. Now, we know that it is the exception that is thrown when an operation does not exist.

The question now is: How are we going to load the operations array? The answer to this question is using a Symfony service configurator. These are special services that allow developers to decouple service logic from the service that provides the required configuration.

Let's take a look at the operation collection configurator:

The Operation Configurator

The operation configurator will hold the necessary code to fill the collection with the operations. It will wrap each operation using a class named "ApiOperation" which receives the operation handler and the operation metadata.

```
namespace App\Api;

use App\Api\Attribute\OperationMetadata;
use App\Api\Operation\OperationInterface;

readonly class ApiOperation {

  public function __construct(
```

CHAPTER 1   CRAFTING INPUTS, OUTPUTS, AND OPERATIONS

```php
    public OperationInterface $handler,
    public OperationMetadata  $metadata
){}
}
```

Now, let's explore how the operation configurator works.

```php
namespace App\Api\Collection;

use App\Api\ApiOperation;
use App\Api\Attribute\OperationMetadata;
use Symfony\Component\DependencyInjection\Attribute\
TaggedIterator;

class OperationCollectionConfigurator {

  public function __construct(
     #[TaggedIterator('api.operation')] private readonly iterable
        $apiOperations
  ){}

  public function configure(OperationCollection
$operationCollection): void
  {
     $operations = [];
     foreach ($this->apiOperations as $operation){
        $metadata = $this->readAttribute(OperationMetadata::class,
        $operation);
        $operations[$metadata->name] = new
        ApiOperation($operation, $metadata);
     }

     $operationCollection->setOperations($operations);
  }
```

```
/**
 * @template T
 * @param class-string<T> $attrClass
 * @return T|null
 */
private function readAttribute(string $attrClass, object
$object)
{
    $reflectionClass = new \ReflectionClass($object);
    $attrs = $reflectionClass->getAttributes($attrClass);
    if(!empty($attrs)) {
      $attr = reset($attrs);
      return $attr->newInstance();
    }

    throw new \RuntimeException(sprintf('Operation class %s has
    no metadata', get_class($object)));
  }
}
```

The configurator service contains a little more code. Let's start with the constructor. It injects a parameter flagged with the TaggedIterator attribute. This attribute loads the **$apiOperations** iterable with all the services tagged as "api.operation", that is, all the operations.

> When we created the OperationInterface, we used the AutoConfigure attribute to tag all services which implemented such interface as "api.operation".

The private **readAttribute** method uses the PHP reflection capabilities to check whether the object passed as a second parameter is marked with the attribute specified with the first parameter. If so, it returns a new instance of the attribute; otherwise, it throws a PHP exception.

The **configure** method loops the operations contained in the "$apiOperations" array. For each one, it gets the metadata using the **readAttribute** method and wraps the operation and its metadata into an **ApiOperation** object. After the loop ends, it sets the operations into the OperationCollection using the **setOperations** method.

We must tell Symfony to use this configurator to configure the OperationCollection service. To achieve it, we have to define it in the services section on the config/services.yaml file.

```yaml
App\Api\Collection\OperationCollection:
 configurator: ['@App\Api\Collection\OperationCollectionConfigurator', 'configure']
```

With the above configuration, Symfony knows that it must use the **OperationCollectionConfigurator** configure method to configure the **OperationCollection** service.

Discovering Operations

Discovering operations is as simple as using the **getOperation** method from the OperationCollection service. Let's create an **ApiOperationHandler** service to encapsulate this logic.

```php
namespace App\Api;

use App\Api\Collection\OperationCollection;
use App\Api\Input\ApiInput;
use App\Api\Output\ApiOutput;

class ApiOperationHandler
{
    public function __construct(
        private readonly OperationCollection $operationCollection,
    ){ }
```

```
public function performOperation(ApiInput $apiInput):
ApiOutput
{
    $operation = $this->operationCollection->
    getOperation($apiInput->operation);
    return $operation->handler->perform($apiInput->data);
}
}
```

The **performOperation** method receives an input model as a parameter. As this model holds the operation name, the method passes it to the OperationCollection **getOperation** method and gets an **ApiOperation** wrapper, which holds the operation handler and the operation metadata. Then, it performs the operation (using the OperationInterface perform method) and returns the result as an ApiOutput model.

Handling NotFoundOperationException Errors

When we wrote the operation collection service, we threw an exception when we did not find an operation. Let's write the class for this exception:

```
use Symfony\Component\HttpKernel\Exception\
NotFoundHttpException;

class NotFoundOperationException extends NotFoundHttpException
{
}
```

The exception class does nothing. It simply extends from the Symfony **NotFoundHttpException**, which automatically sets up the HTTP response code as a "404 Not Found". Now, we need to instruct Symfony to return a formatted JSON response within the missing operation message when

CHAPTER 1   CRAFTING INPUTS, OUTPUTS, AND OPERATIONS

this exception is thrown. To do it, we are going to write a Symfony event subscriber that will keep listening to the Symfony KernelException event. Symfony triggers this event every time an exception is thrown.

```php
namespace App\EventSubscriber;

use App\Exception\NotFoundOperationException;
use Symfony\Component\EventDispatcher\EventSubscriberInterface;
use Symfony\Component\HttpFoundation\JsonResponse;
use Symfony\Component\HttpKernel\Event\ExceptionEvent;
use Symfony\Component\HttpKernel\KernelEvents;

class KernelSubscriber implements EventSubscriberInterface
{
    public static function getSubscribedEvents(): array
    {
        return [
            KernelEvents::EXCEPTION => 'onException'
        ];
    }

    public function onException(ExceptionEvent $event): void
    {
        $exception = $event->getThrowable();
        if($exception instanceof NotFoundOperationException){
            $event->setResponse(new JsonResponse([
                'errors' => [
                    'operation' => $exception->getMessage()
                ]
            ]));
        }
    }
}
```

CHAPTER 1   CRAFTING INPUTS, OUTPUTS, AND OPERATIONS

As you can see in the above code, the **onException** method is executed after the kernel exception event is triggered. This method checks whether the exception thrown is an instance of **NotFoundOperationException**. If so, it creates a JsonResponse with the exception message and it is passed to the event **setResponse** method. Finally, this response is the one that will be returned to the end client.

Conclusion

We have explored the creation of a collection repository that acts as a central hub for storing all defined operations. Additionally, we have introduced a handler responsible for retrieving operations from the collection and executing them. Furthermore, we have addressed the scenario of encountering an operation that does not exist within the collection. By implementing mechanisms to handle "not found" operations gracefully, we can ensure robustness and user-friendliness within our API.

In the next section, we will shift our focus to lazy operations. By leveraging the Symfony lazy loading techniques, we can ensure that our applications remain responsive and efficient, loading only the necessary components when they are needed.

Section 4. Lazy Operations

In the previous section, we learned how to use the **symfony** capabilities to create a collection to store the operations that can be executed within our API. In an environment with plenty of operations available, it's essential to consider the performance implications of loading all operations upfront. This is where lazy operations can come into play.

Lazy operations allow us to defer the loading of operations until they are actually needed. This approach can significantly improve the

CHAPTER 1   CRAFTING INPUTS, OUTPUTS, AND OPERATIONS

performance of our API, especially when dealing with a large number of operations or with operations that are a bit heavy to instantiate.

As an example, we could think about an operation that injects the mailer service. Even when you do not need the mailer, it is always instantiated in order to construct the operation and add it to the collection.

To be able to add lazy operations to the collection, we are relying on the **lazy** parameter of the **Autoconfigure** attribute.

The LazyOperation Interface

The **LazyOperationInterface** code is similar to the OperationInterface code but with the following differences:

- The Autoconfigure attribute sets the parameter **lazy** as true. This means that the operations that implement this interface will be lazy-loaded into the collection.

- It adds a method named **getMetadata** to return the operation metadata. This method is required because metadata attributes cannot be reliably accessed on lazy-loaded (proxied) services.

```
use App\Api\Attribute\OperationMetadata;
use App\Api\Output\ApiOutput;
use Symfony\Component\DependencyInjection\Attribute\Autoconfigure;

#[Autoconfigure(lazy: true, tags: ['api.operation'])]
interface LazyOperationInterface
{
    public function perform(mixed $data): ApiOutput;
    public function getMetadata(): OperationMetadata;
}
```

We have to take into account that lazy operations services cannot be readonly classes nor final classes.

Marking an Operation As Lazy

To mark an operation as lazy, we only have to implement the previous interface.

```php
use App\Api\Attribute\OperationMetadata;
use App\Api\Operation\LazyOperationInterface;
use App\Api\Output\ApiOutput;
use App\Security\Miscelanea\OperationNames;

class SendReportingByEmail implements LazyOperationInterface
{
    public function perform(mixed $data): ApiOutput
    {
        /**
         * Required code to send the reporting by email
         */
        return new ApiOutput([
            'report_id' => '5899865', 'email_status' => 'queued'
        ], 200);
    }

    public function getMetadata(): OperationMetadata
    {
        return new OperationMetadata(
            name: OperationNames::SendReportingByEmail->name,
            input: SendReportingByEmailInput::class
        );
    }
}
```

As we can see, the operation metadata is returned within the **getMetadata** method.

Modifying the OperationCollectionConfigurator

We have to modify the OperationCollectionConfigurator service to check whether an operation is flagged as lazy. If so, it will have to extract the metadata using the **getMetadata** method instead of reading the OperationMetadata attribute.

```php
public function configure(OperationCollection
$operationCollection): void
{
   $operations = [];
   foreach ($this->apiOperations as $operation){
     if($operation instanceof LazyOperationInterface) {
        $metadata = $operation->getMetadata();
        $operations[$metadata->name] = new ApiOperation(
          $operation,
          $metadata
        );
     }
     else{
        $metadata = $this->readAttribute(OperationMetadata:
        :class, $operation);
        $operations[$metadata->name] = new
        ApiOperation($operation, $metadata);
     }
   }
   $operationCollection->setOperations($operations);
}
```

CHAPTER 1   CRAFTING INPUTS, OUTPUTS, AND OPERATIONS

Conclusion

We have used the **lazy** parameter of the **Autoconfigure** attribute so that all the operations that implement the **LazyOperation** interface are loaded in lazy mode. This allows us to improve performance and instantiate heavy operations only when they are executed.

In the next section, we will shift our focus to validation. We will explore strategies for ensuring that incoming requests adhere to the expected requirements, paving the way for reliable and error-free operation execution.

Section 5. Validating Operations

In "Section 1. Request Inputs and Outputs," we discussed defining operations that might require specific parameters for execution. Ensuring these parameters are valid and consistent is crucial to avoiding errors during the operation execution.

This section explores how to leverage Symfony's validation capabilities to achieve this goal.

The Validation Service

Let's start creating a service to encapsulate the validation logic:

```
namespace App\Validation;

use App\Exception\InvalidPayloadException;
use Symfony\Component\Serializer\SerializerInterface;
use Symfony\Component\Validator\Exception\ValidationFailedException;
use Symfony\Component\Validator\Validator\ValidatorInterface;

class ValidationHandler
```

```php
{
    public function __construct(
        private readonly SerializerInterface $serializer,
        private readonly ValidatorInterface $validator
    ){}

    public function deserializeAndValidate(array|string $payload, string $className)
    {
        try{
            $object = (is_array($payload))
                ? $this->serializer->denormalize($payload, $className)
                : $this->serializer->deserialize($payload, $className, 'json')
            ;
        }
        catch(\Symfony\Component\Serializer\Exception\ExceptionInterface $e) {
            throw new InvalidPayloadException();
        }

        $errors = $this->validator->validate($object);
        if(count($errors) > 0) {
            throw new ValidationFailedException(null, $errors);
        }

        return $object;
    }
}
```

This service utilizes two key Symfony components:

- **Symfony Serializer**: The handler first employs the serializer service to transform the incoming request payload into the input model specified in the metadata input parameter. The payload format can be either JSON (encoded string) or an array.

- **Symfony Validator**: Once deserialized, the input model is validated using the Symfony validator service. This ensures the data adheres to pre-defined constraints, guaranteeing consistency and preventing potential errors during operation execution.

If the validation process concludes without errors, the deserialized input model is returned, ready for further processing by the operation handler. In case of validation failures (invalid data), a Symfony **ValidationFailedException** is thrown.

We wrapped deserialization in a try-catch block to handle potential errors such as incorrect data types, missing required fields, or invalid JSON. If any of these issues occur, an **InvalidPayloadException** is thrown instead:

```php
namespace App\Exception;
use Symfony\Component\HttpFoundation\Response;

class InvalidPayloadException extends \RuntimeException
{
    public function __construct(string $msg = 'Malformed or unrecognized payload' , int $code = Response::HTTP_BAD_REQUEST, ?\Throwable $previous = null)
    {
       parent::__construct($msg, $code, $previous);
    }
}
```

CHAPTER 1   CRAFTING INPUTS, OUTPUTS, AND OPERATIONS

The **InvalidPayloadException** simply adds a message that informs that an invalid payload has been sent.

Validating Before Performing the Operation

Let's make some changes to the ApiOperationHandler so that the data is validated before performing the operation.

```
use App\Api\Collection\OperationCollection;
use App\Api\Input\ApiInput;
use App\Api\Output\ApiOutput;
use App\Validation\ValidationHandler;

class ApiOperationHandler
{
   public function __construct(
     private readonly ValidationHandler $validationHandler,
     private readonly OperationCollection $operationCollection,
   ){ }

   public function performOperation(ApiInput $apiInput): ApiOutput
   {
      $operation = $this->operationCollection->
      getOperation($apiInput->operation);

      $inputData = ($operation->metadata->input)
         ? $this->validationHandler->deserializeAndValidate
         ($apiInput->data, $operation->metadata->input)
         : $apiInput->data
      ;

      return $operation->handler->perform($inputData);
   }
}
```

Now, the constructor also injects the ValidationHandler service. The **performOperation** validates the API input data (if the operation's metadata specifies an input model class). If the validation fails, a ValidationFailedException will be thrown and the operation will not be executed.

Handling Deserializing and Validating Errors

As we did for the NotFoundOperationException, we must handle the validation errors exception (**InvalidPayloadException** and **ValidationFailedException**) so that we can return a readable JSON output. Let's modify the KernelSubscriber.

```
namespace App\EventSubscriber;

use App\Exception\InvalidPayloadException;
use App\Exception\NotFoundOperationException;
use Symfony\Component\EventDispatcher\EventSubscriberInterface;
use Symfony\Component\HttpFoundation\JsonResponse;
use Symfony\Component\HttpKernel\Event\ExceptionEvent;
use Symfony\Component\HttpKernel\KernelEvents;
use Symfony\Component\Validator\Exception\ValidationFailedException;

class KernelSubscriber implements EventSubscriberInterface
{
    public static function getSubscribedEvents(): array
    {
        return [
            KernelEvents::EXCEPTION => 'onException',
        ];
    }
```

```php
public function onException(ExceptionEvent $event): void
{
    $exception = $event->getThrowable();
    if($exception instanceof ValidationFailedException){
        $errors = [];
        foreach($exception->getViolations() as $violation) {
            $errors[$violation->getPropertyPath()] =
            $violation->getMessage();
        }

        $event->setResponse( new JsonResponse([
            'errors' => $errors
        ], 400));
        return;
    }

    if($exception instanceof InvalidPayloadException) {
        $event->setResponse( new JsonResponse([
            'payload' => $exception->getMessage()
        ], 400));
        return;
    }

    if($exception instanceof NotFoundOperationException){
        $event->setResponse( new JsonResponse([
            'errors' => [
                'operation' => $exception->getMessage()
            ]
        ], 404));
        return;
    }
}
}
```

CHAPTER 1   CRAFTING INPUTS, OUTPUTS, AND OPERATIONS

We have included two if blocks to deal with the **InvalidPayloadException** and the **ValidationFailedException**. For the **ValidationFailedException**, it loops through the violation constraints and creates an array where the keys are the properties causing an error and the values are the error messages. For the **InvalidPayloadException**, it returns the exception message.

Conclusion

Having established mechanisms for executing operations and ensuring the validity of the incoming payloads, we only have to create the endpoint to receive operation requests.

Section 6. Connecting the Dots: Building an API Endpoint

We have established the core components for handling operation executions. Now, it's time to enable clients to interact with the API. This section focuses on creating a Symfony controller that will serve as an endpoint for receiving operation requests.

By defining a route within this controller, we will establish a designated URL that clients can use to submit operation requests.

Let's explore how this connects the various services we have created to the outside world, allowing our API to handle incoming operation calls.

Creating the Controller

In "Section 1. Request Inputs and Outputs," we learned how to structure our **ApiInput** so that we can encapsulate into it both the operation to be executed and the data required to execute such operation. Although it may seem that our controller must strictly receive the data according to

31

the structure of the **ApiInput** model, this does not have to be the case and, during the rest of the section, we will learn how, with just a little extra code, we can receive the input data in various ways.

Mapping the Received Payload Directly to the ApiInput

This first case is the most obvious. The received payload must exactly match with the **ApiInput** model. The MapRequestPayload attribute internally deserializes the request payload into the model and validates it. If any error is found, Symfony creates a **ValidationFailedException** with the errors, wraps it into an **UnprocessableEntityHttpException**, and throws it with a 422 Unprocessable Entity Http code.

```
use App\Api\ApiOperationHandler;
use App\Api\Input\ApiInput;
use Symfony\Bundle\FrameworkBundle\Controller\AbstractController;
use Symfony\Component\HttpFoundation\JsonResponse;
use Symfony\Component\Routing\Annotation\Route;
use Symfony\Component\HttpKernel\Attribute\MapRequestPayload;

class ApiController extends AbstractController
{
    public function __construct(
        private readonly ApiOperationHandler
        $apiOperationHandler
    ){}

    #[Route('/api/v1/operation', name: 'api_operation',
    methods: ['POST'])]
    public function operationAction(#[MapRequestPayload]
    ApiInput $apiInput): JsonResponse
    {
```

```
        $apiOutput = $this->apiOperationHandler->
        performOperation($apiInput);
        return new JsonResponse($apiOutput->data,
        $apiOutput->code);
    }
}
```

Receiving the Operation Name As a Route Parameter

In this case, the operation name comes within a route parameter name **operationSlug** and the operation data comes within the payload. To handle the request, we need to make some changes:

Get the Operation Name from the Slug

To discover which operation must be executed, let's create a static method in the OperationNames enumeration which will transform the operation slug into an operation name.

```
use function Symfony\Component\String\u;

// .......

public static function getBySlug(string $slug): string
{
    return u($slug)->camel()->title();
}
```

The **getBySlug** function uses the Symfony String "u" function to camelize the slug and uppercase the first character. In this way, we manage to convert the slug into a valid operation name.

CHAPTER 1   CRAFTING INPUTS, OUTPUTS, AND OPERATIONS

Create the ApiInput Model Manually

In the below code, we are going to create the ApiInput model following the next steps:

- We ensure that the received payload is a valid JSON. This is mandatory since we do not use the **MapRequestPayload** attribute in this case.
- We use the **getBySlug** function to get the operation name and use it as the first **ApiInput** constructor argument.
- We decode the received payload (the operation data) to an array and use it as the second **ApiInput** constructor argument.

Let's create a method to ensure that the received payload is a valid JSON in the ValidationHandler class:

```
class ValidationHandler
{
    public function __construct(
        private readonly SerializerInterface $serializer,
        private readonly ValidatorInterface $validator
    ){}

    // The other methods

    public function validateAndGetJsonInput(string $content): array
    {
        $data = json_decode($content, true);
        if(is_null($data)){
            if(json_last_error() !== JSON_ERROR_NONE) {
```

CHAPTER 1   CRAFTING INPUTS, OUTPUTS, AND OPERATIONS

```
                throw new InvalidPayloadException('Invali
                    d Json Payload');
            }
            $data = [];
        }
        return $data;
    }
}

#[Route('/api/v1/operation/{operationSlug}', name: 'api_slug_
operation', methods: ['POST'])]
public function operationActionSlug(string $operationSlug,
Request $request, ValidationHandler $validationHandler):
JsonResponse
{
    $data = $validationHandler->
    validateAndGetJsonInput($request->getContent());
    $apiInput = new ApiInput(
        OperationNames::getBySlug($operationSlug),
        $data
    );

    $apiOutput = $this->apiOperationHandler->
    performOperation($apiInput);
    return new JsonResponse($apiOutput->data, $apiOutput->code);
}
```

   The second **ApiInput** parameter (which holds the operation data) received the json decoded data is there are no errors. Remember that this data is validated by the **performOperation** method according to the operation input model. To validate it, it uses the ValidationHandler service from the previous chapter.

CHAPTER 1   CRAFTING INPUTS, OUTPUTS, AND OPERATIONS

Using a Route per Operation Without a Slug Parameter

This case is similar to the previous one, but instead of sending the operation slug as a parameter, the route defines the operation name. In this way, we would facilitate the generation of documentation while keeping our API oriented towards operations.

```
#[Route('/api/v1/operation/send-payment', name: 'api_send_
payment_operation', methods: ['POST'])]
public function operationActionSendPayment(Request $request,
ValidationHandler $validationHandler): JsonResponse
{
    $data = $validationHandler->validateAndGetJsonInput
    ($request->getContent());

    $apiInput = new ApiInput(
        OperationNames::SendPayment->name,
        $data
    );

    $apiOutput = $this->apiOperationHandler->
    performOperation($apiInput);
    return new JsonResponse($apiOutput->data, $apiOutput->code);
}
```

Using an Http Get Route

Http Get requests usually receive the data within the URL query string, so to be able to get the data and pass it to the ApiInput model, we can rely on the Symfony Request query parameter.

```
#[Route('/api/v1/operation/get-campaigns', name: 'api_send_get_
campaigns', methods: ['GET'])]
```

CHAPTER 1   CRAFTING INPUTS, OUTPUTS, AND OPERATIONS

```
public function operationActionGetCampaigns(Request $request):
JsonResponse
{
 $apiInput = new ApiInput(
 OperationNames::GetCampaigns->name,
 $request->query->all()
 );

 $apiOutput = $this->apiOperationHandler->
 performOperation($apiInput);
 return new JsonResponse($apiOutput->data, $apiOutput->code);
}
```

Passing Data Within Route Parameters

This can be situations when some parameters are passed as a route parameters instead of using the query string or the request payload. Let's observe the following example.

```
#[Route('/api/v1/sensor/{sensorId}/operation/update-data',
name: 'api_update_sensor_data', methods: ['PATCH'])]
public function operationActionUpdateSensorData(int $sensorId,
Request $request, ValidationHandler $validationHandler):
JsonResponse
{
    $data = $validationHandler->
    validateAndGetJsonInput($request->getContent());
    $apiInput = new ApiInput(
      OperationNames::UpdateSensorData->name,
      array_merge(
      $data,
              ['sensorId' => $sensorId]
      )
    );
```

37

CHAPTER 1   CRAFTING INPUTS, OUTPUTS, AND OPERATIONS

```
    $apiOutput = $this->apiOperationHandler->performOperation
    ($apiInput);
    return new JsonResponse($apiOutput->data,
    $apiOutput->code);
}
```

In this case, we need to manually add the **sensorId** parameter to the received payload, which is achieved using the PHP array_merge function.

As an improvement, instead of hardcoding the **sensorId** parameter name, we could create an enumeration to hold those parameter names.

```
enum OperationParametersNames: string
{
    case SensorId = 'sensorId';
}
```

And then, we would change the array_merge with this:

```
array_merge(
    json_decode($request->getContent(), true),
    [OperationParametersNames::SensorId->value => $sensorId]
)
```

Combining with Traditional CRUD Routes

In the same way that we can define our endpoints in various ways to receive the operation to be executed and the data, we can also combine operation-oriented routes with traditional CRUD routes.

```
#[Route('/api/v1/template')]
class ApiTemplatingController extends AbstractController
{
    public function __construct(
        private readonly ApiOperationHandler $apiOperationHandler
```

CHAPTER 1   CRAFTING INPUTS, OUTPUTS, AND OPERATIONS

```
    ){}

    #[Route('', name: 'api_get_templates', methods: ['GET'])]
    public function getTemplates(): JsonResponse
    {
        return new JsonResponse([]);
    }

    #[Route('/operation', name: 'api_template_operation',
    methods: ['POST'])]
    public function operationAction(#[MapRequestPayload]
    ApiInput $apiInput): JsonResponse
    {
        $apiOutput = $this->apiOperationHandler-
        >performOperation($apiInput);
        return new JsonResponse($apiOutput->data,
        $apiOutput->code);
    }
}
```

As we can see in the above controller, it combines a CRUD-type endpoint (**getTemplates**) with an operation-oriented endpoint (**operationAction**).

Conclusion

In this section, we have learned how to build an endpoint in different ways so that clients can connect to our API and execute operations. In the next chapter, we will study how to create versions of our API so that we can allow one or more operations to be available only for one or more versions of the API.

CHAPTER 1   CRAFTING INPUTS, OUTPUTS, AND OPERATIONS

Section 7. Versioning the API

It is normal when developing APIs to add new functionalities and operations, and it is also normal that some of those new functionalities are only available for certain versions. In this section, we will explore a way to specify that an operation can only be available for one or more versions.

A New Metadata Parameter

The operation metadata is the perfect place to specify which versions the operation is available in. To achieve this, let's add a new parameter to the attribute.

```
#[\Attribute(\Attribute::TARGET_CLASS)]
class OperationMetadata
{
    public function __construct(
        public readonly string $name,
        public readonly ?array $version = null,
        public readonly ?string $input = null
    ){ }
}
```

The "version" parameter specifies which API versions can execute the operation. If no version is specified, it will mean that no version is required. Now, we need to receive the API version in some way. This way can be using a symfony route parameter.

Receiving the Version

The below code adds a "version" parameter to the controller route.

CHAPTER 1   CRAFTING INPUTS, OUTPUTS, AND OPERATIONS

```
#[Route('/api/{version}/operations', name: 'post_api_
operation', methods: ['POST'])]
public function operationAction(string $version,
#[MapRequestPayload] ApiInput $apiInput): JsonResponse
{
    $apiOutput = $this->apiOperationHandler-
    >performOperation($apiInput, $version);
    return new JsonResponse($apiOutput->data,
$apiOutput->code);
}
```

The "version" parameter arrives as a route parameter. Then, this parameter is passed to the ApiOperationHandler so that it can check internally whether the version matches with the operation.

Checking the Version

Now, it's time to add some modifications to the ApiOperationHandler to be able to check the version.

```
public function performOperation(ApiInput $apiInput, ?string
$version = null): ApiOutput
{
    $operation = $this->operationCollection-
>getOperation($apiInput->operation);

    if(!is_null($version) && $operation->metadata->version &&
!in_array($version, $operation->metadata->version)) {
            OperationDoesNotSupportApiVersionException(sprintf(
              'Operation supported version: %s - Using version: %s',
              implode(",", $operation->metadata->version),
              $version
```

41

CHAPTER 1   CRAFTING INPUTS, OUTPUTS, AND OPERATIONS

```
        ));
    }
    $inputData = ($operation->metadata->input)
        ? $this->validationHandler->
        deserializeAndValidate($apiInput->data, $operation->
        metadata->input)
        : null
    ;

    $operation->handler->perform($inputData);
}
```

The **performOperation** method now receives the "version" as an optional parameter. Then, the method checks the following conditions:

- A version is passed.
- The operation metadata holds a version.
- The version passed does not exist into the operation allowed versions array.

If the above conditions are met, an **OperationDoesNotSupportApiVersionException** is thrown, informing the client that the operation cannot be executed for that API version. Let's see the exception code.

namespace App\Exception;

class OperationDoesNotSupportApiVersionException **extends** \
RuntimeException
{
}

CHAPTER 1   CRAFTING INPUTS, OUTPUTS, AND OPERATIONS

This exception does nothing. We are simply going to check for it in the KernelSubscriber to inform the user about a version error within the JSON response.

Checking for an OperationDoesNotSupportApiVersionException in the KernelSubscriber

As we did in the last sections, we have to check for a version error in the kernel subscriber and format the error correctly.

```
if($exception instanceof
OperationDoesNotSupportApiVersionException){
    $event->setResponse( new JsonResponse([
        'errors' => [
            'operation_version' => $exception->getMessage()
        ]
    ], 400));
    return;
}
```

As you can see, we have only been added another condition for this kind of exception.

Conclusion

In this section, we have extended the **OperationMetadata** attribute by adding a new parameter that specifies the API versions an operation supports. In the final section, we will see how to leverage Symfony's Monolog Bundle together with its events system to automatically log every API request and response.

43

CHAPTER 1   CRAFTING INPUTS, OUTPUTS, AND OPERATIONS

Section 8. Monitoring Operations

Another critical aspect to consider when developing APIs (regardless of the approach) is how to monitor their performance. For example:

- How long does an operation take to process?
- Which operations generate the most bottlenecks?
- What is the error rate (4xx/5xx) for each operation or endpoint?
- What percentage of requests exceed an acceptable latency threshold (e.g., the 95th percentile)?

There are many tools which allow DevOps to monitor APIs such as Prometheus + Grafana, ELK (Elastic/Logstash/Kibana), OpenTelemetry, etc.

In this chapter, we will not cover how to set up external monitoring tools. Instead, we will focus on using Symfony's built-in features to generate log files containing detailed execution data. Later on, developers and DevOps engineers can feed those logs into any monitoring platform to build dashboards and analyze the results.

Creating a Monolog Handler

In Section 3 Prerequisites of the previous chapter, we learned how to install the Monolog bundle: the de facto standard for logging in Symfony applications. Its configuration lives in the *config/packages/monolog.yaml* file. Below is an example that defines a custom handler writing to a dedicated log file:

```
monolog:
    handlers:
        operations_performance:
```

CHAPTER 1   CRAFTING INPUTS, OUTPUTS, AND OPERATIONS

```
            type: stream
            path: "%kernel.logs_dir%/op_performance.log"
            level: debug
            channels: [op_performance]
    channels:
        - deprecation # Deprecations are logged in the
        dedicated "deprecation" channel when it exists
        - op_performance
```

Here, the *operations_performance* handler listens on the *op_performance* channel and writes every debug-level (and above) record to the *var/log/op_performance.log* file (the default location of the %kernel.logs_dir% variable). Since recent Symfony releases include automatic service registration, the kernel dynamically creates a service for each Monolog custom channel that you configure. The service ID is derived from the handler's channel name, converted to camelCase, and suffixed with the "Logger" string. In this example, the service becomes $opPerformanceLogger.

Creating a Logging Wrapper to Log Operations Execution Information

In this section, we are going to explore how to inject the logger configured in the previous section and how to use it to write to the configured file.

```
use Psr\Log\LoggerInterface;
use Symfony\Component\Uid\Uuid;

class OperationPerformanceLogger
{
    public function __construct(
        private readonly LoggerInterface $opPerformanceLogger
    ){}
```

```php
    public function logStartOperation(string $operation, ?array
    $inputData): string
    {
        $id = Uuid::v4();
        $this->opPerformanceLogger->info(json_encode([
            'operation' => $operation,
            'id' => $id,
            'input_data' => $inputData ?? [],
            'ts_start' => microtime(true)
        ]));

        return (string)$id;
    }

    public function logEndOperation(string $operation, string
    $id, int $responseCode, ?array $outputData): void
    {
        $this->opPerformanceLogger->info(json_encode([
            'operation' => $operation,
            'id' => $id,
            'output_data' => $outputData ?? [],
            'ts_end' => microtime(true),
            'response_code' => $responseCode
        ]));
    }
}
```

Let's start within the constructor. As you can see, we have injected the *$opPerformanceLogger* service, which implements the "Psr\Log\LoggerInterface" required by the Symfony's kernel. This service exposes two key methods:

- **logStartOperation**: This method should be invoked when an operation request is received. It takes the

CHAPTER 1   CRAFTING INPUTS, OUTPUTS, AND OPERATIONS

operation name and an array of input values (or an empty array if none) and writes the following information (as JSON) to the log file:

- **operation**: The operation name
- **id**: An id to identify the request. Here, we use Symfony Uid component to generate an Uuid v4 as an ID.
- **input_data**: The received input data as an array or an empty array if no input data has been received.
- **ts_start**: The timestamp when the operation has been received.

This method returns the generated id. In the next sections, we will learn how to carry this id within the request so that it can be used to log the operation termination data.

- **logEndOperation**: This method should be invoked after the operation requested execution ends and the response has been sent to the client. It receives the operation name, the id generated in the **logStartOperation** method, the http response code returned to the client and the execution result data. The method writes the following information in the log file:
  - **operation**: The operation name.
  - **id**: An id to identify the request. It is the same ID generated in the **logStartOperation** method.
  - **output_data**: The output data array or an empty array if no response data is returned to the client. This could be the case of a 204 No Content Http Response.

47

- **ts_end**: The timestamp when the operation ends.
- **response_code**: The http response code returned to the client.

With this logger service in place, you can leverage Symfony's event system to automatically record both the start and end of each API operation.

Writing to the Log When an Operation Request Is Received

We are going to use the **kernelEvents.REQUEST** Symfony event to discover whether an operation request has been received and, if so, write to the log. To achieve that, we will create a new Symfony Kernel Subscriber:

```
use App\Api\Input\ApiInput;
use App\Api\Logger\OperationPerformanceLogger;
use Symfony\Component\EventDispatcher\EventSubscriberInterface;
use Symfony\Component\HttpKernel\Event\RequestEvent;
use Symfony\Component\HttpKernel\KernelEvents;
use Symfony\Component\Serializer\Exception\ExceptionInterface;
use Symfony\Component\Serializer\SerializerInterface;

class OperationPerformanceSubscriber implements EventSubscriberInterface
{
    public const string OP_REQ_ATTR = 'OP_REQ';

    public function __construct(
        private readonly SerializerInterface $serializer,
        private readonly OperationPerformanceLogger
        $operationPerformanceLogger
    ){}
```

CHAPTER 1 CRAFTING INPUTS, OUTPUTS, AND OPERATIONS

```php
    public static function getSubscribedEvents(): array
    {
        return [
            KernelEvents::REQUEST   =>
['onOperationReceived', 2]
        ];
    }

    public function onOperationReceived(RequestEvent
$event): void
    {
        $uri = $event->getRequest()->getUri();
        if(!preg_match('#\/api\/v[1-9]{1}\/operation#',
        $uri)) {
            return;
        }

        try{
            $apiInput = $this->serializer->deserialize($event-
            >getRequest()->getContent(), ApiInput::class, 'json');
            if(!empty($apiInput->operation)) {
                $operationRequestId = $this-
                >operationPerformanceLogger-
                >logStartOperation($apiInput->operation,
                $apiInput->data);
                $event->getRequest()->attributes->set(self::OP_
                REQ_ATTR, $operationRequestId . ':' .
                $apiInput->operation);
            }
        }
        catch(ExceptionInterface $e) {}
    }
}
```

Let's explore the above new subscriber. This subscriber keeps listening to the **KernelEvents::REQUEST** event and, after catching it, it executes the **onOperationReceived** method. This method performs the following logic:

- It checks whether the request URI matches the operation request route path.
- If do not, it returns and performs no extra logic.
- If so, it deserializes the payload to the **ApiInput** model.
- If the are no errors in the deserializing process, the method uses the **logStartOperation** method from the **OperationPerformanceLogger** service to write the operation requested information. Then, it gets the $operationRequestId returned by the **logStartOperation** method and saves it into the request attributes bag so that we can use it later.

As you have noticed, there is no code in the **onOperationReceived** catch block. This is because if there are any errors after validating the received API input payload, the client will receive a 400 Bad Request response and the request will not continue to the handler, so it is not worth writing in the log in this case.

Writing to the Log When an Operation Request Ends

Finally, we just have to write to the log after an operation request ends. To achieve that, we will rely on the Symfony **KernelEvents. TERMINATE** event.

```
use App\Api\Input\ApiInput;
use App\Api\Logger\OperationPerformanceLogger;
use Symfony\Component\EventDispatcher\EventSubscriberInterface;
```

CHAPTER 1   CRAFTING INPUTS, OUTPUTS, AND OPERATIONS

```php
use Symfony\Component\HttpKernel\Event\RequestEvent;
use Symfony\Component\HttpKernel\Event\TerminateEvent;
use Symfony\Component\HttpKernel\KernelEvents;
use Symfony\Component\Serializer\Exception\ExceptionInterface;
use Symfony\Component\Serializer\SerializerInterface;

class OperationPerformanceSubscriber implements EventSubscriberInterface
{
 public const string OP_REQ_ATTR = 'OP_REQ';

 public function __construct(
 private readonly SerializerInterface $serializer,
 private readonly OperationPerformanceLogger
$operationPerformanceLogger
 ){}

 public static function getSubscribedEvents(): array
 {
 return [
 KernelEvents::REQUEST   => ['onOperationReceived', 2],
            KernelEvents::TERMINATE => 'onOperationTerminated'
        ];
    }

    public function onOperationReceived(RequestEvent $event): void
    {
        $uri = $event->getRequest()->getUri();
        if(!preg_match('#^\/api\/v[1-9]{1}\/operation#', $uri)) {
            return;
        }
```

CHAPTER 1   CRAFTING INPUTS, OUTPUTS, AND OPERATIONS

```
        try{
            $apiInput = $this->serializer->deserialize($event->
            getRequest()->getContent(), ApiInput::class, 'json');
            if(!empty($apiInput->operation)) {
                $operationRequestId = $this-
                >operationPerformanceLogger-
                >logStartOperation($apiInput->operation,
                $apiInput->data);
                $event->getRequest()->attributes->set(self::OP_
                REQ_ATTR, $operationRequestId . ':' .
                $apiInput->operation);
            }
        }
        catch(ExceptionInterface $e) {}
    }

    public function onOperationTerminated(TerminateEvent
    $event): void
    {
        $opReqAttr = $event->getRequest()->attributes->
        get(self::OP_REQ_ATTR);
        if($opReqAttr) {
            list($opId, $opName) = explode(':', $opReqAttr);
            $responseArray = ($event->getResponse()->
            getContent())
                ? json_decode($event->getResponse()->
                getContent(), true)
                : []
            ;

            $responseCode = $event->getResponse()->
            getStatusCode();
```

```
            $this->operationPerformanceLogger->
            logEndOperation($opName, $opId, $responseCode,
            $responseArray);
        }
    }
}
```

Let's analyze now the **onOperationTerminated** event. It proceeds as follows:

- It checks whether the request attributes bag contains a value for a key named "OP_REQ". If so, it means that a request operation has been logged within the REQUEST event and now we have to log the termination.

- It explodes the **$opReqAttr** using the ":" token string to get both the operation ID and the operation name values.

- It creates the response array by applying the PHP json_decode function to the received response content or as a **null** value if no response content has been sent to the client.

- It gets the http response code.

- Finally, it writes the termination information to the log using the **OperationPerformanceLogger logEndOperation** method.

Conclusion

In this chapter, we have constructed the core functionalities of our operation-oriented API. We have established a robust foundation by

- Defining clear models for operation inputs and outputs
- Defining a concrete way to create operation services (OperationInterface and OperationMetadata)
- Lazy-loading operations that can be heavy to instantiate
- Implementing a centralized collection for storing operations and a dedicated handler to efficiently retrieve and execute them
- Validating operations data using a dedicated validation handler, safeguarding the API against invalid payloads
- Crafting the endpoints that serve as the entry points for all API requests, streamlining user interaction and request handling
- Combining the Symfony monolog bundle and the Symfony event system to log an operation request reception and an operation request termination so that we can use that information later for analyzing our API system health

With these core functionalities in place, our API is equipped to handle various operations and deliver the desired functionality. However, security remains paramount. In the next chapter, we will shift our focus to fortifying both the endpoint and individual operations, ensuring a secure API environment.

CHAPTER 2

Securing Operations

In this section, we will use the Symfony security features to protect both the endpoints and the operations. To protect the endpoints, we will use the Symfony firewall system through which we will establish the user authentication mechanism. Then, we will rely on Symfony voters to grant or deny an operation execution based on certain rules.

Section 1. The User

In this section, we are going to create the user entity, which will serve us to store the users who can access the API. Then we will start the database we configured in "Section 3. Prerequisites" in the Bookfront matter and load users on it.

The User Entity

We are going to use the Symfony maker command to create our entity. To do it, we need to execute the following command in the project root folder:

```
bin/console make:entity
```

CHAPTER 2 SECURING OPERATIONS

Create a string field named token, another named email, and a JSON field named roles (JSON fields require a platform that supports them, such as PostgreSQL and MySQL 5.7+):

- The token field will hold the token, which will be used to authenticate the user in the rest of the chapter.
- The email field will be used as an identifier.
- The roles field will hold the user roles. We will use this field to authorize certain roles to execute an operation using Symfony voters.

After the command finishes, you can see a new user class under the *src/Entity* folder. This should look like this:

```
namespace App\Entity;

use App\Repository\UserRepository;
use Doctrine\ORM\Mapping as ORM;

#[ORM\Entity(repositoryClass: UserRepository::class)]
class User
{
    #[ORM\Id]
    #[ORM\GeneratedValue]
    #[ORM\Column]
    private ?int $id = null;

    #[ORM\Column(length: 255)]
    private ?string $token = null;

    #[ORM\Column(length: 255)]
    private ?string $email = null;

    #[ORM\Column]
    private array $roles = [];
```

```php
public function getId(): ?int
{
    return $this->id;
}

public function getToken(): ?string
{
    return $this->token;
}

public function setToken(string $token): static
{
    $this->token = $token;

    return $this;
}

public function getEmail(): ?string
{
    return $this->email;
}

public function setEmail(string $email): static
{
    $this->email = $email;

    return $this;
}

public function getRoles(): array
{
    return $this->roles;
}

public function setRoles(array $roles): static
```

CHAPTER 2   SECURING OPERATIONS

```
    {
        $this->roles = $roles;

        return $this;
    }
}
```

We have now to make our User entity implement the Symfony UserInterface. Implementing this interface is required for Symfony's authentication system to recognize the User entity as a valid user.

```
namespace App\Entity;

use App\Repository\UserRepository;
use Doctrine\ORM\Mapping as ORM;
use Symfony\Component\Security\Core\User\UserInterface;

#[ORM\Entity(repositoryClass: UserRepository::class)]
class User implements UserInterface
{
    // ... other methods goes here

    public function eraseCredentials()
    {

    }

    public function getUserIdentifier(): string
    {
        return $this->getEmail();
    }
}
```

As our entity already defines the **getRoles** method since it is an entity property, we have to define the other two methods required by the interface:

CHAPTER 2   SECURING OPERATIONS

- **eraseCredentials**: We can use this method to clear sensitive information stored in this object. We leave it empty because we are not storing temporary sensitive data like plaintext passwords.

- **getUserIdentifier**: We use this method to return the user identifier, that is, the email.

Loading the Database with Users

Thanks to the Symfony Fixtures Bundle, we can create classes that act as database loader services. These services must be located under the *src/DataFixtures* folder and must extend the *Doctrine\Bundle\FixturesBundle\Fixture* class. Let's create a Fixture class for loading users on the User entity:

```php
namespace App\DataFixtures;

use App\Entity\User;
use Doctrine\Bundle\FixturesBundle\Fixture;
use Doctrine\Persistence\ObjectManager;

class UserFixtures extends Fixture
{
    public function load(ObjectManager $manager): void
    {
        $user = new User();
        $user->setToken('vWvn1GOu2Lx5foFgQrRp');
        $user->setRoles(['ROLE_USER']);
        $user->setEmail('spiderman@avengers.com');

        $user2 = new User();
        $user2->setToken('zPLhK8iQqg9fg7u5jnp');
        $user2->setRoles(['ROLE_SENDER']);
```

```
            $user2->setEmail('captain-america@avengers.com');
            $manager->persist($user);
            $manager->persist($user2);
            $manager->flush();
        }
}
```

The **load** method receives the Doctrine **ObjectManager** service as a parameter. Inside the method, we create two users, one with the ROLE_USER and another one with the ROLE_SENDER. Then, we use the **ObjectManager persist** and **flush** methods to save them to the database.

To execute the fixtures and load the users to the database, we must execute the following commands:

```
bin/console doctrine:schema:create
bin/console doctrine:fixtures:load
```

> The first command only needs to be executed once. It creates the database schema so that the next command can load the rows successfully. If you created the database before, you must drop it before creating it again by using the *doctrine:schema:drop* command. Consider using Doctrine migrations in a real environment.

After the command finishes, we already have our user table loaded, and we are ready to start the next section.

Conclusion

In this section, we have created the User entity which represents the database-stored users who can access our API. In the next section, we will create a Symfony firewall which will protect our API endpoint and only grant access to authenticated users.

CHAPTER 2   SECURING OPERATIONS

Section 2. Protecting the Endpoint

To ensure that only authenticated users can access our API endpoint, we are going to implement a token-based authentication using a custom Symfony authenticator. It will extract the token from the request header, validate it, and, if the token is valid, the user will be successfully authenticated; otherwise, an authentication failure will be returned to the client.

The Operation Authenticator

The authenticator service extends the class AbstractAuthenticator, which implements the AuthenticatorInterface. All authenticators must implement this interface. The AbstractAuthenticator defines the **createToken** method, which must fit most use cases. Below you can see the authenticator code:

```
namespace App\Security;

use Symfony\Component\HttpFoundation\JsonResponse;
use Symfony\Component\HttpFoundation\Request;
use Symfony\Component\HttpFoundation\Response;
use Symfony\Component\Security\Core\Authentication\Token\
TokenInterface;
use Symfony\Component\Security\Core\Exception\
AuthenticationException;
use Symfony\Component\Security\Core\Exception\
CustomUserMessageAuthenticationException;
use Symfony\Component\Security\Http\Authenticator\
AbstractAuthenticator;
use Symfony\Component\Security\Http\Authenticator\Passport\
Badge\UserBadge;
```

CHAPTER 2 SECURING OPERATIONS

```php
use Symfony\Component\Security\Http\Authenticator\Passport\
Passport;
use Symfony\Component\Security\Http\Authenticator\Passport\
SelfValidatingPassport;

class ApiTokenAuthenticator extends AbstractAuthenticator
{
    public function supports(Request $request): ?bool
    {
        return $request->headers->has('X-AUTH-TOKEN') || preg_
        match('#\/api\/v1#', $request->getUri());
    }

    public function authenticate(Request $request): Passport
    {
        $apiToken = $request->headers->get('X-AUTH-TOKEN');
        if (empty($apiToken)) {
            throw new CustomUserMessageAuthenticationException(
            'No API token provided');
        }

        return new SelfValidatingPassport(new
        UserBadge($apiToken));
    }

    public function onAuthenticationSuccess(Request $request,
    TokenInterface $token, string $firewallName): ?Response
    {
        return null;
    }

    public function onAuthenticationFailure(Request $request,
    AuthenticationException $exception): JsonResponse
```

```
    {
        $data = [
            'message' => strtr($exception->getMessageKey(),
            $exception->getMessageData())
        ];

        return new JsonResponse($data, Response::HTTP_
        UNAUTHORIZED);
    }
}
```

Let's go through the authenticator methods step by step:

- **supports**: It decides whether the authenticator will be processed or not. The authenticator will be executed if the X-AUTH-TOKEN header has been sent or the request URI matches the */api/v1* pattern. By implementing this approach, we can effectively handle requests that do not include a token without compromising security.

- **authenticate**: First, it checks whether the token is empty. If so, it throws an exception. Otherwise, it returns a SelfValidatingPassport with the API token as a badge. After returning, the security bundle will check whether the token is registered or not.

When configuring the User Provider, we will understand how the security layer validates the token.

- **onAuthenticationSuccess**: It is only executed when the authentication succeeds. It would be used, for instance, to update a user's valid login counter. In this case, we will leave it empty so that the process can continue.

- **onAuthenticationFailure**: It is only executed when the authentication fails. In this case, it returns a JSON response with an authentication error message and a *401 Unauthorized* code.

The Firewall and the User Provider

Both the firewall and the user provider must be defined in the Symfony *config/packages/security.yaml* file. Let's show it:

The User Provider

We are using the entity-user-provider as a user provider.

```
security:

  # .......

providers:
  users_provider:
    entity:
      class: App\Entity\User
      property: token
```

This provider uses the doctrine bundle to search on the User entity for a user whose token matches the token sent within the request headers. After the **authenticate** method returns the **SelfValidatingPassport**, the security layer will use this provider to check whether the token is valid or not.

The Firewall

The Firewall will protect all requests whose URI matches the *^/api/v1* pattern. It will authenticate users using the ApiTokenAuthenticator and the users to compare with will be loaded using the provider configured in the previous section.

```yaml
firewalls:
    # Other firewalls
    api:
        pattern: '^/api/v1'
        provider: users_provider
        stateless: true
        custom_authenticators:
            - App\Security\ApiTokenAuthenticator
```

The *stateless* parameter indicates whether the firewall should be stateless or stateful. When set to *true*, it indicates that Symfony will not store the user's authentication information in the session. This is useful when authenticating an API within a token since the token is sent within the headers on every request.

Conclusion

We have achieved that only authorized users with valid credentials will be granted access to the API by using a Symfony authenticator. In the next section, we will extend our security measures beyond the endpoint to encompass individual operations. We'll explore the utilization of Symfony voters, a flexible authorization system within Symfony.

Section 3. Protecting the Operations

Our endpoint is now protected and only authenticated users can execute operations, so the next security goal is to enable the protection of those operations that require it. For example, some operations might only be executed by users with a specific role. To achieve this goal, we are going to use Symfony voters.

The Abstract Operation Voter

Let's start by writing an abstract operation voter that the rest of the operation voters will have to extend.

```php
use App\Api\ApiOperation;
use Symfony\Component\Security\Core\Authorization\Voter\Voter;

abstract class OperationVoter extends Voter {
    protected function supports(string $attribute, mixed $subject): bool
    {
        return ($attribute === 'PERFORM' && $subject instanceof ApiOperation);
    }
}
```

The **supports** method adds common logic for all voters which extends it. It checks that the attribute parameter holds the value "PERFORM" and that the subject parameter is an instance of the **ApiOperation** class. These couple of checks make sense, taking into account the current operation-oriented context:

- We always check that the attribute holds the value "PERFORM" since we always want to perform an operation.

- We always check that the subject is an **ApiOperation** instance so that we can check the operation name in the child class.

The Operation Voter

As we said in the previous section, an operation voter will have to extend from the abstract operation voter and implement the authorization logic. Let's create a voter for the SendPayment operation which ensures that the authenticated user holds the "ROLE_SENDER" role.

```php
use App\Security\Miscelanea\OperationNames;
use Symfony\Component\Security\Core\Authentication\Token\TokenInterface;

class SendPaymentVoter extends OperationVoter
{
    protected function supports(string $attribute, mixed $subject): bool
    {
        if(parent::supports($attribute, $subject) && $subject->metadata->name === OperationNames::SendPayment->name){
            return true;
        }

        return false;
    }

    protected function voteOnAttribute(string $attribute, mixed $subject, TokenInterface $token): bool
    {
        if(!in_array('ROLE_SENDER', $token->getUser()->getRoles())) {
            return false;
        }

        return true;
    }
}
```

The **supports** method checks the attribute and the subject instance using the parent logic and also checks that the operation name is "SendPayment". If the supports method returns "true," Symfony will execute the **voteOnAttribute** method and check if the user holds the ROLE_SENDER role. If the user roles do not match the required ones, a 403 Forbidden response will be returned, and the operation execution will be halted.

There could be situations where a set of operations share the same authorization rules. In this case, the same voter could authorize that set of operations. To achieve this, the voter **supports** method should check that the requested operation is part of that set. As an example, let's imagine we have an operation named "ApprovePayment" and both "SendPayment" and "ApprovePayment" operations can only be performed by the ROLE_SENDER. We could create a new static method called "getPaymentOperations" in the OperationNames enum from Chapter 1. This method should return an array containing the ROLE_SENDER allowed operations, and the voter should check whether the requested operation is contained in that array.

```
enum OperationNames
{
    case SendPayment;
    case ApprovePayment;

    public static function getPaymentOperations(): array
    {
        return [
            self::ApprovePayment->name,
            self::SendPayment->name
        ];
    }
}
```

As we can see, the *getPaymentOperations* method returns the allowed operations. Now in the voter, we should use it in the **supports** method:

```
use App\Security\Miscelanea\OperationNames;
use Symfony\Component\Security\Core\Authentication\Token\TokenInterface;

class SenderVoter extends OperationVoter
{
    protected function supports(string $attribute, mixed $subject): bool
    {
        if(parent::supports($attribute, $subject) && in_array($subject->metadata->name, OperationNames::getPaymentOperations())){
            return true;
        }

        return false;
    }

    protected function voteOnAttribute(string $attribute, mixed $subject, TokenInterface $token): bool
    {
        if(!in_array('ROLE_SENDER', $token->getUser()->getRoles())) {
            return false;
        }

        return true;
    }
}
```

The above voter would grant access to all the operations contained in the array returned by the **getPaymentOperations** as long as the user's role is "ROLE_SENDER".

There is an extra configuration we have to set up before checking the voter. Since we do not know if any voter is going to be executed or not, in the event that none have been executed, it would be considered that all voters have abstained. When this situation occurs, Symfony consults the security configuration parameter "*allow_if_all_abstain*", which by default is "false." We must change the value of this parameter to "true" since we want Symfony to allow us to execute the operation when no voter has been executed. If you want to query more information about the access decision strategy, you can read more in the security symfony docs.

We can change this configuration by setting the new value in the *config/packages/security.yaml* file:

```yaml
security:
    access_decision_manager:
        strategy: unanimous
        allow_if_all_abstain: true
```

Handling Access Denied Errors

Symfony's Security HTTP component monitors security errors through an exception listener. To tailor the "operation denied" response, we need to create a custom subscriber. This subscriber must be executed before the default security listener. We can achieve this by assigning a higher priority to our custom **AccessDeniedSubscriber**.

```php
use Symfony\Component\EventDispatcher\EventSubscriberInterface;
use Symfony\Component\HttpFoundation\JsonResponse;
use Symfony\Component\HttpKernel\Event\ExceptionEvent;
use Symfony\Component\HttpKernel\KernelEvents;
```

```php
use Symfony\Component\Security\Core\Exception\
AccessDeniedException;

class AccessDeniedSubscriber implements
EventSubscriberInterface
{
    public static function getSubscribedEvents(): array
    {
        return [
            KernelEvents::EXCEPTION => ['onException', 2]
        ];
    }

    public function onException(ExceptionEvent $event): void
    {
        $exception = $event->getThrowable();
        if (!$exception instanceof AccessDeniedException) {
            return;
        }

        $event->setResponse(new JsonResponse(
            [ 'authorization' => $exception->getMessage()],
            403
        ));
    }
}
```

There are two important aspects in the above subscriber that we must pay attention to:

- The subscriber's priority is set to 2. This allows it to intercept "access denied" exceptions first and customize the response.

CHAPTER 2　SECURING OPERATIONS

- The subscriber ignores exceptions that are not instances of the **AccessDeniedException**. This is because these other errors will be handled by the KernelSubscriber as detailed in Chapter 1.

Checking for Permission

In this section, we're modifying the ApiOperationHandler so that it checks whether the user has enough permissions for operating.

```
use App\Api\Collection\OperationCollection;
use App\Api\Input\ApiInput;
use App\Api\Output\ApiOutput;
use App\Validation\ValidationHandler;
use Symfony\Bundle\SecurityBundle\Security;
use Symfony\Component\Security\Core\Exception\
AccessDeniedException;

class ApiOperationHandler
{
    public function __construct(
        private readonly ValidationHandler $validationHandler,
        private readonly OperationCollection
        $operationCollection,
        private readonly Security $security
    ){ }

    public function performOperation(ApiInput $apiInput):
    ApiOutput
    {
        $operation = $this->operationCollection->
        getOperation($apiInput->operation);
```

```
    $isGranted = $this->security->isGranted('PERFORM',
    $operation);
    if(!$isGranted){
        throw new AccessDeniedException('Not allowed to
        perform this operation');
    }

    $inputData = ($operation->metadata->input)
        ? $this->validationHandler->
        deserializeAndValidate($apiInput->data, $operation->
        metadata->input)
        : null
    ;

    return $operation->handler->perform($inputData);
    }
}
```

Let's focus on the changes below the "getOperation" line. It uses the method **isGranted** of the **security.helper** Symfony service to check whether the user has permissions or not. Internally, this method executes all the voters whose **supports** method returns true. As the voters work under a "unanimous" strategy, if any voter denies access, then the requested operation will be revoked; otherwise, it will be granted.

> To use the "security.helper" service, we inject it using the "Symfony\Bundle\SecurityBundle\Security" class which is an alias of it.

Conclusion

We have achieved fine-grained control over operation access by using voters. This ensures that only authorized users can execute specific operations, safeguarding sensitive data and functionalities within the

API. In the next section, we will address scenarios where operations require access to information about the currently logged-in user.

Section 4. Accessing the Logged User from Operations

There can be operations that could require access to the user-logged data. For instance, the SendPayment operation could need the current user's balance before sending the payment. For this reason, we need a way to

- Know whether an operation requires access to the user
- Pass the user to the operation so that it can use it

The OperationRequiresUserInterface

Let's start by creating an interface that will be implemented by those operations that require access to the user.

```
use Symfony\Component\Security\Core\User\UserInterface;

interface OperationRequiresUserInterface
{
    public function setUser(UserInterface $user): void;
}
```

This interface declares a method named **setUser**, which will be used by the ApiOperationHandler to pass the user to the operation.

Passing the User to the Operation

We have to modify the ApiOperationHandler **performOperation** method so that it can check whether the operation requires the user and pass it.

CHAPTER 2   SECURING OPERATIONS

```php
public function performOperation(ApiInput $apiInput): ApiOutput
{
    $operation = $this->operationCollection->
    getOperation($apiInput->operation);
    $isGranted = $this->security->isGranted('PERFORM',
    $operation);
    if(!$isGranted){
        throw new AccessDeniedException('Not allowed to perform
        this operation');
    }
    $inputData = ($operation->metadata->input)
        ? $this->validationHandler->deserializeAndValidate
        ($apiInput->data, $operation->metadata->input)
        : null
    ;
    if($this-security-getToken()?-getUser() && $operation->
    handler instanceof OperationRequiresUserInterface) {
        $operation->handler->setUser($this->security->
        getToken()->getUser());
    }
    $operation->handler->perform($inputData);
}
```

After validating the operation data, the **performOperation** function checks whether the operation object is an instance of **OperationRequiresUserInterface**, that is, the operation implements that interface. If so, the handler uses the **setUser** method to pass the user to the operation.

75

CHAPTER 2   SECURING OPERATIONS

Implementing the OperationRequiresUserInterface

Let's make the SendPayment operation to implement the **OperationRequiresUserInterface**.

```
use App\Api\Attribute\OperationMetadata;
use App\Api\Input\Operation\SendPaymentInput;
use App\Api\Output\ApiOutput;
use App\Security\Miscelanea\OperationNames;
use Symfony\Component\Security\Core\User\UserInterface;

#[OperationMetadata(
    name: OperationNames::SendPayment->name,
    input: SendPaymentInput::class,
)]
class SendPaymentOperation implements OperationInterface,
OperationRequiresUserInterface
{

    private ?UserInterface $user = null;

    /**
     * @param SendPaymentInput $data
     */
    public function perform(mixed $data): ApiOutput
    {
        /**
         * Business logic to send the payment would go here
         */
          return new ApiOutput([
            'id' => '77fg76hf'
        ], 202);
    }
```

```
    public function setUser(?UserInterface $user): void
    {
        $this->user = $user;
    }
}
```

As you can see, the **setUser** method initializes the operation **user** property with the user passed as a parameter and, from that moment, the user is available to be used in the operation.

Conclusion

In this section, we have designed a way to allow operations to access the currently logged user if they require it. In the next section, we will learn how to validate input requests according to the user role.

Section 5. Validating Operations According to the User Role

In the previous chapter, we validated the operations according to the operation input class properties constraints. In this chapter, we are going to go one step further and validate them based on the user's role too.

Using Validation Groups in the Input Model

Symfony Validation Groups are a great feature to validate an object only against some of its constraints. Let's start from the following assumption: We want to create an operation for creating projects. These projects always require a name and a description. The project start and end dates will be required only for the ROLE_PROJECT_MANAGER user so that:

- **ROLE_PROJECT_MANAGER**: They will have to send all the parameters.
- **ROLE_DEVELOPER**: They will only have to send the name and the description.

Below you can see the input class:

```php
use Symfony\Component\Validator\Constraints\IsNull;
use Symfony\Component\Validator\Constraints\Date;
use Symfony\Component\Validator\Constraints\NotBlank;

readonly class CreateProjectInput
{
    public function __construct(
        #[NotBlank(message: 'name cannot be empty', groups:
        ['ROLE_PROJECT_MANAGER', 'ROLE_DEVELOPER'])]
        public string $name,
        #[NotBlank(message: 'description cannot be empty',
        groups: ['ROLE_PROJECT_MANAGER', 'ROLE_DEVELOPER'])]
        public string $description,
        #[NotBlank(message: 'start date cannot be empty',
        groups: ['ROLE_PROJECT_MANAGER'])]
        #[IsNull(message: 'start date must be empty', groups:
        ['ROLE_DEVELOPER'])]
        #[Date(message: 'start date must be a valid date',
        groups: ['ROLE_PROJECT_MANAGER'])]
        public string $startDate,
        #[NotBlank(message: 'end date cannot be empty', groups:
        ['ROLE_PROJECT_MANAGER'])]
        #[IsNull(message: 'end date must be empty', groups:
        ['ROLE_DEVELOPER'])]
```

```
            #[Date(message: 'end date must be a valid date',
            groups: ['ROLE_PROJECT_MANAGER' ])]
            public string $endDate,
    ){}
}
```

As you can observe, the model specifies that both name and description are required for both managers and developers, but start and end dates can only be specified by the project managers. In fact, an IsNull constraint specifies that developers cannot fill those properties.

> We use the **IsNull** constraint to avoid generating errors in the database caused by trying to store empty strings on date nullable fields.

Specifying That the Operation Uses Groups

Now, we need to specify that the operation uses validation groups so that the handler can act accordingly. To do it, we are going to add a new parameter named "validateByRole" in the OperationMetadata attribute so that the ApiOperationHandler can know whether to use validation groups or not.

```
#[\Attribute(\Attribute::TARGET_CLASS)]
class OperationMetadata
{
 public function __construct(
                public readonly string $name,
        public readonly ?string $version = null,
        public readonly ?string $input = null,
        public readonly ?bool $validateByRole = null
    ){ }
}
```

CHAPTER 2   SECURING OPERATIONS

Adapting the Validation Handler to Use Groups

If you remember from Chapter 1, "Section 5. Validating Operations," we created a class named **ValidationHandler** to deserialize and validate the received operation data according to the operation input model. We need to modify this class so that it can apply the validation groups when needed.

Let's take a look to the **ValidationHandler** class again:

```
use App\Exception\InvalidPayloadException;
use Symfony\Component\Serializer\SerializerInterface;
use Symfony\Component\Validator\Exception\ValidationFailedException;
use Symfony\Component\Validator\Validator\ValidatorInterface;

class ValidationHandler
{
    public function __construct(
        private readonly SerializerInterface $serializer,
        private readonly ValidatorInterface $validator
    ){}

    public function deserializeAndValidate(array|string $payload, string $className, ?array $groups)
    {
        try{
            $object = (is_array($payload))
                ? $this->serializer->denormalize($payload, $className)
                : $this->serializer->deserialize($payload, $className, 'json')
            ;
        }
        catch(\Symfony\Component\Serializer\Exception\ExceptionInterface $e) {
```

CHAPTER 2　SECURING OPERATIONS

```
        throw new InvalidPayloadException();
    }

    $errors = $this->validator->validate($object, null,
    $groups);
    if(count($errors) > 0) {
        throw new ValidationFailedException(null, $errors);
    }

    return $object;
    }
}
```

As you can see, we have only made two changes:

- We have added a third parameter to the **deserializeAndValidate** method to be able to pass the groups to apply. It may be null since groups may not apply.

- We pass the groups to the Symfony validation service. Symfony also accepts the groups parameter as null for the cases where groups do not apply.

Adapting the ApiOperationHandler to Pass the Groups

To finish this section, we must instruct the ApiOperationHandler so that it can know whether to use validation groups or not.

```
public function performOperation(ApiInput $apiInput): ApiOutput
{
    $operation = $this->operationCollection->
    getOperation($apiInput->operation);
```

```
    $isGranted = $this->security->isGranted('PERFORM',
    $operation);
    if(!$isGranted){
        throw new AccessDeniedException('Not allowed to perform
        this operation');
    }

    $validationGroups = ($operation->metadata->validateByRole)
? $this->security->getUser()->getRoles() : null;
    $inputData = ($operation->metadata->input)
        ? $this->validationHandler->deserializeAndValidate
        ($apiInput->data, $operation->metadata->input,
        $validationGroups)
        : $apiInput->data
    ;

    return $operation->handler->perform($inputData);
}
```

If we take a look to the **ApiOperationHandler performOperation** method, it checks the "validateByRole" value. If it is true, it assigns an array for the "$validationGroups" variable which holds the group names (which match the user roles). Otherwise, it assigns null. Then, the "$validationGroups" variable is passed to the **deserializeAndValidate** method as the third parameter.

Conclusion

We have explored how to use symfony validation groups to validate a subset of the operation input properties based on the authenticated user roles. This offers us the flexibility to enforce different validation rules tailored to the specific permissions and responsibilities of each user role.

In the next section, we will learn how to use a rate limiter to control the frequency of requests made by each user to prevent abuse and ensure system stability.

Section 6. Controlling Requests

To prevent DoS attacks, we will rely on the Symfony rate-limiter component to control the number of requests that arrive at the API.

The Token-Bucket Strategy

Imagine a token bucket as a container that holds a limited number of tokens. In the context of rate-limiting requests to an API, the token bucket strategy works like this:

- Initially, the token bucket is filled with a certain number of tokens.
- Each time a request is made to the API, the system checks if there are enough tokens in the bucket.
- If there are enough tokens available, the request execution continues, and the system removes a token from the bucket.
- If there are not enough tokens available, the request is delayed until more tokens become available.

Over time, the token bucket refills at a certain rate, adding new tokens to the bucket.

CHAPTER 2   SECURING OPERATIONS

Configuring Token-Bucket Strategy

The rate limiter configuration is located in the file *config/packages/framework.yaml* under the *rate_limiter* section.

```
framework:
    rate_limiter:
        api:
            policy: 'token_bucket'
            limit: 5000
            rate: { interval: '20 minutes', amount: 200 }
```

The above configuration allows a maximum of 5000 tokens and adds 200 tokens every 20 minutes after making the first HTTP request. The policy key indicates that we are using the token_bucket strategy. As we are using service auto-wiring, Symfony will create a bound var named "apiLimiter" which will hold our rate-limiter service. Let's see how to use it in the next section.

Using the Limiter

We will use the apiLimiter service within the subscriber we created in Chapter 1. Concretely, we are going to listen to the Symfony KernelRequest event to check whether we can continue with the request, that is, there are tokens available. This way, we can check the limit before the call arrives at the controller.

```
use App\Exception\InvalidPayloadException;
use App\Exception\NotFoundOperationException;
use App\Validation\ValidationHandler;
use Symfony\Component\EventDispatcher\EventSubscriberInterface;
use Symfony\Component\HttpFoundation\JsonResponse;
use Symfony\Component\HttpKernel\Event\ExceptionEvent;
```

```php
use Symfony\Component\HttpKernel\Event\RequestEvent;
use Symfony\Component\HttpKernel\KernelEvents;
use Symfony\Component\RateLimiter\RateLimiterFactory;
use Symfony\Component\Validator\Exception\
ValidationFailedException;
use  Symfony\Component\RateLimiter\Exception\
RateLimitExceededException;
class KernelSubscriber implements EventSubscriberInterface
{

 public function __construct(
 private readonly ValidationHandler $validationHandler,
 private readonly RateLimiterFactory $apiLimiter
 ){}

 public static function getSubscribedEvents(): array
 {
 return [
 KernelEvents::EXCEPTION => 'onException',
 KernelEvents::REQUEST => 'onKernelRequest'
 ];
 }

 public function onKernelRequest(RequestEvent $event): void
 {
 $limiter = $this->apiLimiter->create($event->getRequest()->
getClientIp());
 $limiter->consume()->ensureAccepted();
    }

    public function onException(ExceptionEvent $event): void
    {
        $exception = $event->getThrowable();
```

```php
if($exception instanceof ValidationFailedException){
    $errors = [];
    foreach ($exception->getViolations() as
    $violation) {
        $errors[$violation->getPropertyPath()] =
        $violation->getMessage();
    }

    $event->setResponse(new JsonResponse([
        'errors' => $errors
    ], 400));
    return;
}

if($exception instanceof RateLimitExceededException) {
    $event->setResponse(new JsonResponse([
        'error' => 'Api Rate limit exceeded'
    ], 429));
    return;
}

if($exception instanceof InvalidPayloadException) {
    $event->setResponse(new JsonResponse([
        'error' => $exception->getMessage()
    ], 400));
    return;
}

if($exception instanceof NotFoundOperationException){
    $event->setResponse(new JsonResponse([
        'errors' => [
            'operation' => $exception->getMessage()
        ]
```

```
            ], 400));
            return;
        }
    }
}
```

The **onKernelRequest** method gets the limiter by using the *apiLimiter* service and checks whether the request is accepted. If not, it throws a RateLimitExceededException. We also check for this exception on the **onException** method and return a *429 Too Many Requests* HTTP code to the client.

Conclusion

As a plus to finish this chapter, we have added an extra security layer that helps us to prevent DoS attacks by setting a limit to the requests that the API can handle by using a token-bucket strategy. In the next chapter, we will delve into the utilization of Symfony messenger, a robust tool within the Symfony framework, to enable asynchronous execution of large operations, that is, operations that can take some time to be processed.

CHAPTER 3

Background Execution of API Operations

So far, we have learned how to manage operations through a single endpoint, how to secure our endpoint using a Symfony firewall, and how to grant or deny access to our operations using Symfony voters. In this chapter, we will learn how to execute operations in the background so that the client does not have to wait until the operation is performed. This is useful for operations that can take some time to be executed. Our *SendPayment* operation would be a good example since it would probably connect to a payment provider to send the money. As we do not know how much time this kind of connection can take, it is preferable to execute it in the background and send a notification to the client (can be an email, SMS, or push notification, among others) after the operation finishes.

CHAPTER 3 BACKGROUND EXECUTION OF API OPERATIONS

Section 1. Marking Operations As Background

We created the OperationMetadata attribute in Chapter 1 to store the following data related to the operation:

- The operation name
- The class-name, which holds the parameters the operation requires to be performed
- Whether we have to pass roles as groups to the validation process or not

Let's add a new parameter to the attribute class which will indicate whether the operation must be executed in the background or not.

```php
readonly class Background
{
    /**
    * Delay in seconds before the background operation is
      executed
    */
    public function __construct(
        public ?int $delay = null
    ){ }
}

#[\Attribute(\Attribute::TARGET_CLASS)]
class OperationMetadata
{
    public function __construct(
        public readonly string $name,
        public readonly ?string $input = null,
        public readonly ?bool $useValidationGroups = null,
```

CHAPTER 3   BACKGROUND EXECUTION OF API OPERATIONS

```
        public readonly ?Background $background = null
    ){ }
}
```

As the background execution could be delayed, we create first a **Background** class which contains a delay parameter that can be null. If provided, the operation will be executed in the background adding an extra delay. The **OperationMetadata** holds now a new Background type parameter. If provided, the operation must be sent to the background instead of being executed in real-time.

Now, if we would want to mark the SendPayment operation as background, we simply would have to add the background parameter to the attribute.

```
#[OperationMetadata(
    name: OperationNames::SendPayment->name,
    input: SendPaymentInput::class,
    useValidationGroups: false,
    background: new Background(300)
)]
class SendPaymentOperation implements OperationInterface
{
    // Rest of the methods
}
```

In the above example, we indicate that the **SendPayment** operation will be executed in the background and its execution will be delayed 300 seconds (5 minutes).

Conclusion

We have extended the existing OperationMetadata attribute by adding a new parameter that allows us to indicate whether a specific operation should be executed in the background. By setting this flag, we signal that the operation's execution can be asynchronous and decoupled from the user's immediate request. In the next section, we will explore how to create the operation message, its corresponding handler, and the magic behind connecting them using the Symfony AsMessageHandler attribute.

Section 2. The Operation Message and Handler

We are going to use the Symfony messenger component to execute operations in the background. First of all, we have to create a message class and a handler for the message.

Creating the Operation Message

```
use Symfony\Component\Security\Core\User\UserInterface;

class OperationMessage
{
    public function __construct(
        public readonly string $operation,
        public readonly mixed $operationInput,
        public readonly ?string $userIdentifier
    ){ }
}
```

The message class holds in the constructor the necessary parameters to execute an operation: the operation name, the operation data, and the user identifier (if required by the operation). Let's code now the message handler.

> As we will see in the next section, we will use the **getUserIdentifier** method from our User entity to set the value of the **OperationMessage** user parameter. This method returns the user email.

Creating the Operation Handler

Now, we need a handler to manage the **OperationMessage** messages.

```
use App\Api\Collection\OperationCollection;
use App\Api\Operation\OperationRequiresUserInterface;
use Symfony\Component\Messenger\Attribute\AsMessageHandler;
use Doctrine\ORM\EntityManagerInterface;

#[AsMessageHandler]
class OperationMessageHandler
{
    public function __construct(
        private readonly OperationCollection
        $operationCollection,
        private readonly EntityManagerInterface $em
    ){ }

    public function __invoke(OperationMessage $message): void
    {
        $apiOperation = $this->operationCollection->
        getOperation($message->operation);
        if($message->user && $apiOperation->handler instanceof
        OperationRequiresUserInterface) {
            $user = $this->em->getRepository(User::class)->
            findOneByEmail($message->userIdentifier);
            if(!$user){
                    throw new \InvalidArgumentException("Unk
                    own user while executing operation: " .
                    $message->operation);
            }
            $apiOperation->handler->setUser($user);
        }
```

```
        $apiOperation->handler->perform($message->
        operationInput);
    }
}
```

The handler __invoke function behaves in a similar way that the ApiOperationHandler does. It gets the operation to execute from the collection, checks whether it requires setting the user and sets it if so. Finally, it performs the operation. If the user is required, the handler retrieves first the user from the database and then passes it to the operation. Since **getUserIdentifier()** in the user entity returns the user's email, we use **findOneByEmail()** to retrieve the user from the database in the background handler.

Conclusion

We have created the operation message and its corresponding handler so that, after dispatching an operation message to the background, it can be handled successfully. In the next section, we will bridge the gap between our existing ApiOperationHandler to check whether an operation requires background processing based on the previously introduced flag in the OperationMetadata attribute.

Section 3. Sending Operations to the Background

So far, we have put in place the mechanisms to mark operations as background and to deal with those enqueued operations (the message and its handler). Now, we need our ApiOperationHandler to be able to check whether an operation must be sent to the background. Let's modify it to add this functionality.

```php
use App\Api\Collection\OperationCollection;
use App\Api\Input\ApiInput;
use App\Api\Operation\OperationRequiresUserInterface;
use App\Api\Output\ApiOutput;
use App\Messenger\OperationMessage;
use App\Validation\ValidationHandler;
use Symfony\Bundle\SecurityBundle\Security;
use Symfony\Component\Messenger\MessageBusInterface;
use Symfony\Component\Messenger\Stamp\DelayStamp;
use Symfony\Component\Security\Core\Exception\
AccessDeniedException;

class ApiOperationHandler
{
 public function __construct(
 private readonly ValidationHandler $validationHandler,
 private readonly OperationCollection $operationCollection,
        private readonly Security $security,
        private readonly MessageBusInterface $bus
    ){ }

    public function performOperation(ApiInput $apiInput): ApiOutput
    {
        $operation = $this->operationCollection->
        getOperation($apiInput->operation);
        $isGranted = $this->security->isGranted('PERFORM',
        $operation);
        if(!$isGranted){
            throw new AccessDeniedException('Not allowed to
            perform this operation');
        }
```

```
                $validationGroups = ($operation->metadata->
                    useValidationGroups) ? [$this->security->
                    getUser()->getRoles()] : null;
    $inputData = ($operation->metadata->input)
        ? $this->validationHandler-
        >deserializeAndValidate($apiInput->data,
        $operation→metadata→input, $validationGroups)
        : null
;

$userIdentifier = null;
$user = null;
if($operation->handler instanceof
OperationRequiresUserInterface) {
    $user = $this->security->getToken()->getUser();
    $userIdentifier = $user->getUserIdentifier();

}

if($operation->metadata->background) {
    // Multiply delay * 1000 since DelayStamp expects
        delay in miliseconds
    $stamps = ($operation->metadata->background->delay)
    ? [new DelayStamp($operation->metadata->background->
    delay * 1000)] : [];
    $this->bus->dispatch( new
    OperationMessage($operation->metadata->name,
    $inputData, $userIdentifier), $stamps);
      return new ApiOutput(['status' =>
      'queued'], 202);
}
if($user){
```

```
            $operation->handler->setUser($user);
        }
        return $operation->handler->perform($inputData);
    }
}
```

Let's examine the changes that we have introduced:

- The constructor injects the **MessageBusInterface** service, which allows us to send an operation to the background (we will learn in the next chapter how to route messages to the corresponding transport).

- After ensuring the operation can be performed, its data is valid and whether the user is required, the handler figures out whether the operation must be sent to the background by checking if the operation metadata holds the background parameter, that is, it is not null. If so, the handler proceeds as follows:

    - It checks whether it must add a delay by looking at the background delay value. If a delay has been specified, it creates a DelayStamp passing the specified delay (We multiply the delay by 1000 since the DelayStamp constructor receives the delay in milliseconds).

    - It creates the operation message and dispatches it using the bus service.

    - It returns the corresponding output within a *202 Accepted* code, which indicates that the requested operation has been accepted and will be executed later.

As the ApiOperationHandler validates the operation parameters and checks the authorization rules before queueing the operation, we have not to make these checks again in the message handler.

Conclusion

We have explored how to modify the handler to identify operations flagged for background processing and leverage the Symfony Messenger bus service to enqueue them. However, ensuring efficient background processing requires proper configuration. In the next section, we will learn how to configure the system to route background operation execution messages to a designated transport.

Section 4. Routing Operations

With everything done so far, if we send a request to execute an operation marked as background, it won't be queued. That's because we need to configure the most important part, that is, routing operation messages to a transport.

The transport configuration is placed in the *config/packages/messenger.yaml* file. Below, we are showing how to configure the Redis server we installed in "Section 3. Prerequisites" in the Bootfront matter as a transport and how to instruct messenger to route operation messages to that transport.

```
framework:
  messenger:
    transports:
      operations:
        dsn: '%env(MESSENGER_TRANSPORT_DSN)%'
    routing:
      App\Messenger\OperationMessage: 'operations'
```

As we can see, the "transports" section shows the available transports. In this case, there is only a Redis transport created, which uses as dsn the one from the *.env* file. The routing section specifies which messages are routed to which transports. In this case, the OperationMessage will be routed to the *operations* transport.

Consuming Messages

Once the transport is ready, the operations sent to the background won't be executed immediately. Instead, they will be queued and wait for a dedicated process called **worker** to handle them. These workers run continuously in the background, waiting for new operations to arrive in the queue. Symfony messenger comes with a useful command called **messenger:consume** to start a worker and keep them consuming messages. Let's see how we would consume messages from the **operations** transport:

```
bin/console messenger:consume operations
```

We should not keep consumers running forever since they could consume more memory over time. To avoid this, we can use the following command options to control how much time the worker is alive:

- **time-limit**: It is used to specify how much time the worker will be alive (in seconds).
- **message-limit**: It is used to specify how many messages will be consumed before dying.

```
bin/console messenger:consume operations --time-limit=3600
```

The above command starts a worker which will keep consuming from **operations** transport for an hour. After passing an hour it will be killed.

Chapter 3   Background Execution of API Operations

Managing Workers

As our workers should be killed after a certain time, we should use a tool which can raise the workers again so they are continuously consuming from the queues. Supervisor is an easy-to-use tool that can help to achieve this. You can install supervisor via the following command:

```
sudo apt-get install supervisor
```

After installation, we must write the required config so that our operation workers can start after every reset. Supervisor configuration normally lives in the */etc/supervisor/conf.d* directory. We could create a file named "operations.conf" in that folder with the following configuration:

/etc/supervisor/conf.d/operations.conf

```
[program:messenger-consume]
command=php /path/to/your/app/bin/console messenger:consume operations --time-limit=3600
user=<your_user>
numprocs=4
startsecs=0
autostart=true
autorestart=true
startretries=5
process_name=%(program_name)s_%(process_num)02d
```

Let's review the above configuration key by key:

- **command**: It is the command that Supervisor will handle, in our case the operation execution worker.

- **user**: It is the operating system user who executes the command.

- **numprocs**: The number of processes (workers) that will be executed.

CHAPTER 3   BACKGROUND EXECUTION OF API OPERATIONS

- **autostart**: It indicates whether the command is initialized automatically (we must set it to true since we want our workers to be automatically started).

- **autorestart**: It indicates whether the command is restarted automatically (we must set it to true since we want our workers to automatically restart after every 3600 seconds).

- **startretries**: It indicates how many times Supervisor will try to start the process after failure.

- **process_name**: It indicates a format to build the process name.

Checking the Transport Works

To check that an operation performing is queued for later processing, we are going to modify the SendPayment metadata attribute to flag it as background. As we learned in "Section 1. Marking Operations As Background," we must set the operation metadata background parameter with a new Background class instance.

Now, let's request the operation endpoint to execute a **SendPayment** operation. As it is flagged as background, the endpoint should queue it using the Redis transport and return a 202 Accepted code.

Request:

```
curl --request POST \
  --url http://127.0.0.1:8000/api/v1/operation \
  --header 'Content-Type: application/json' \
  --header 'X-AUTH-TOKEN: zPLhK8iQqg9fg7u5jnp' \
  --data '{
    "operation" : "SendPayment",
```

```
    "data" : {
        "receiver" : "8528f744fg788",
        "amount" : 56.87
    }
}'
Response:

202 Accepted
{
    "status": "queued"
}
```

So far, the operation is queued, but it will not be performed after a worker starts. Before starting a worker, let's ensure the operation has been successfully routed to the Redis transport. To do it, we can log into the Redis server and check the operations stream contents. We can log into the Redis server in two ways:

- Accessing into the docker-container and then accessing into the redis shell using the **redis-cli** command (the container comes with the **redis-cli** command installed).

- Accessing directly using the linked port (Requires installing **redis-cli**).

Let's use option 1. To access the container, open a terminal and execute the following command:

```
docker exec -it <your_container_name> sh
```

After being prompted into the container, we have to log into the Redis server. This is as simple as running the next command:

```
redis-cli
```

Then, when we are logged into the Redis server. We can run the next order to check the length of the operations stream:

```
xlen operations
```

Note "operations" refers to the stream name as defined in the messenger transport configuration.

The above command should return a length of 1, which would tell us that the operation has been routed successfully. Finally, we only have to start a worker and ensure it processes the operation. Let's execute the messenger:consume command and observe how the operation is executed.

```
bin/console messenger:consume operations -vv
```

After executing the worker, we should see the following output:

```
[OK] Consuming messages from transport "operations".

// The worker will automatically exit once it has received a
stop signal via the messenger:stop-workers command.

// Quit the worker with CONTROL-C.
[info] Received message App\Messenger\OperationMessage
[info] Message App\Messenger\OperationMessage handled by App\
Messenger\OperationMessageHandler::__invoke
[info] App\Messenger\OperationMessage was handled successfully
(acknowledging to transport).
```

As we can see, the *info* logs inform us that the operation has been handled successfully.

Retrying Failed Operations

By default, if handling a message fails three times, Symfony will discard it. You can change these parameters using the *max_retries* option as follows:

```
framework:
  messenger:
    transports:
      operations:
        dsn: '%env(MESSENGER_TRANSPORT_DSN)%'
        retry_strategy
          max_retries 2
```

As shown in the above config, we would indicate Symfony messenger to retry 2 times instead of 3. To avoid permanent message loss in case of failure, we must configure a failure transport. When Symfony messenger detects a configured failure transport, it will route the failed messages to that transport so that they can be retried later as long as the error that caused the failure has been fixed. Let's see how to configure it:

```
framework:
  messenger:
    failure_transport: failed
    transports:
      operations:
        dsn: '%env(MESSENGER_TRANSPORT_DSN)%'
        retry_strategy
          max_retries 2
        failed 'doctrine://default?table_name=failed_operations'
```

Now, after an operation handling fails, Symfony will not discard it but it will route the failed message to the failed transport. The failed transport uses doctrine as a backend so that the operation message will be stored in a table named *failed_operations* in our database. Later, we can consume those messages as we would do with any other transport.

> Symfony provides a set of commands to retry messages from the failure transport. You can read more here: `https://symfony.com/doc/current/messenger.html`.

Conclusion

In this section, we have learned how to set up the right configuration to route operation messages to a Redis transport. We have also explored how to check that an operation has been successfully routed checking the corresponding Redis key and we finally have run a worker to execute the operation. As a plus, we have shown how to use Supervisor to manage our workers and restart them.

In the next section, we will see how to create separated queues for routing operations depending on its priority.

Section 5. Prioritizing Operations

There can be situations where the volume of operations that must be sent to the background is too high. In these cases, it may be interesting to choose to segment the volume of operations by queues based, for example, on priority. This is what we are going to implement in this section. To achieve this, we will rely on the Symfony Prioritized Transports feature.

Defining the Priorities

To define the available operation priorities, let's create an enum for holding them:

```
enum Priority
{
    case NORMAL;
    case HIGH;
}
```

For simplicity, the enum holds two cases that represent the priorities: **NORMAL** and **HIGH**.

Modifying the Metadata Attribute

Now, we need to add a new parameter to the Background class attribute so that we can flag an operation with a specified priority.

```
class Background
{
    public function __construct(
        public readonly ?int $delay = null,
        public readonly ?Priority $priority = Priority::NORMAL
    ){ }
}
```

As you can see, the **Background** class constructor takes a Priority enum case as a second constructor argument. By default, all background operations hold a NORMAL priority.

Creating a Message for the HIGH Priority Operations

The operations with a NORMAL priority will be routed using the existing OperationMessage message class. If we remember from "Section 4. Routing Operations," after dispatching an OperationMessage, it is routed to the operations transport. In order to separate NORMAL and HIGH operations, we must route them to diferent transports, so first of all, we need a new message class for HIGH priority messages:

```
use App\Messenger\OperationMessage;

class HighPriorityOperationMessage extends OperationMessage
{
}
```

As both NORMAL priority operations and HIGH priority ones hold the same parameters, we can simply extend the existing **OperationMessage** class.

Creating a Transport for Each Priority

As we want to separate operations by priority in different transports, we need to make some changes in the transports configuration.

```
framework:
  messenger:
    transports:
      operations:
        dsn: '%env(MESSENGER_TRANSPORT_DSN)%'
        options:
          group: 'normal'
      operations_high
```

```
            dsn '%env(MESSENGER_TRANSPORT_DSN)%'
            options
                group 'high'
    routing
        App\Messenger\OperationMessage 'operations'
        App\Messenger\HighPriorityOperationMessage
        'operations_high'
```

Let's take a look to the new configuration.

- There are two transports:
  - **operations**: For routing operations with NORMAL priority
  - **operations_high**: For routing operations with HIGH priority

- Each option sets the group parameter. When using the Symfony redis-transport, you can use the group parameter under the "options" section to set the priority. Symfony internally uses the Redis streams groups and consumers features to achieve it.

- Each message will be routed to its corresponding transport.

Modifying the Message Handler

The message handler should be able to handle both kind of messages. Symfony messenger allows us to achieve this by using the **AsMessageHandler** attribute at the method level instead of using it at the class level.

```
class OperationMessageHandler
{
    public function __construct(
```

CHAPTER 3   BACKGROUND EXECUTION OF API OPERATIONS

```php
    private readonly OperationCollection
    $operationCollection,
    private readonly EventDispatcherInterface
    $eventSubscriber,
    private readonly EntityManagerInterface $em
){ }

#[AsMessageHandler]
public function handleNormalPriorityOperations(OperationMessage $message): void
{
    $this->handleMessage($message);
}

#[AsMessageHandler]
public function handleHighPriorityOperations(HighPriorityOperationMessage $message): void
{
    $this->handleMessage($message);
}

private function handleMessage(OperationMessage|HighPriorityOperationMessage $message): void
{
    $apiOperation = $this->operationCollection->
    getOperation($message->operation);
    $user = null;
    if($message->user && $apiOperation->handler instanceof
    OperationRequiresUserInterface) {
        $user = $this->em->getRepository(User::class)->findOneByEmail($message->user);
        $apiOperation->handler->setUser($user);
    }
```

CHAPTER 3 BACKGROUND EXECUTION OF API OPERATIONS

```
        $apiOperation->handler->perform($message->
        operationInput);
    }
}
```

As you can see in the code above, we create a method named **handleNormalPriorityOperations** to handle NORMAL operations and another one named **handleHighPriorityOperations** to handler the HIGH ones. Since both methods execute the same code, we have moved the handler code to a private method named **handleMessage**.

Dispatching the Message Depending on the Priority

Here, we have to come back to the previous sections. There, we modified the ApiOperationHandler class to check whether we had to queue the operation execution or not. Now, we need to modify it again to check the operation priority and use the corresponding message class.

```
if($operation->metadata->background) {
    $stamps = ($operation->metadata->background->delay)
        ? [new DelayStamp($operation->metadata->background->
        delay * 1000)]
        : []
    ;

    $message = ($operation->metadata->background->priority ===
    Priority::NORMAL)
        ? new OperationMessage($operation->metadata->name,
        $inputData, $userIdentifier)
        : new HighPriorityOperationMessage($operation-
        >metadata->name, $inputData, $userIdentifier)
    ;
```

110

CHAPTER 3   BACKGROUND EXECUTION OF API OPERATIONS

```
    $this->bus->dispatch($message, $stamps);
        return new ApiOutput(['status' => 'queued'], 202);
}
```

As you can see above, after checking the metadata delay parameter, we create an "OperationMessage" message class for NORMAL priority operations or a "HighPriorityOperationMessage" for HIGH priority operations.

Conclusion

In this section, we have learned how to use symfony messenger capabilities to balance operation messages between queues based on a priority parameter. This allows us to prioritize certain operation executions so that they could take too much to have to wait for other operations to be processed.

In the next chapter, we will use the Symfony event system to dispatch an event after a background operation finishes.

Section 6. Triggering Post-Execution Notifications

Some operations could require that users be notified after the operation execution finishes. For instance, after sending a payment, the user could receive an email or an SMS with information about the payment process.

We are going to implement the post-execution notifications only for the background operations because, as the user does not know when the operation will end, it would be useful to inform them about it.

Marking an Operation to Send a Notification

Since not all operations would need to send a notification, we need a way to specify that an operation requires sending a notification after being processed. Let's add a new parameter to the OperationMetadata attribute to specify that the operation requires sending a notification.

```
#[\Attribute(\Attribute::TARGET_CLASS)]
class OperationMetadata
{
  public function __construct(
        public readonly string $name,
        public readonly ?string $version = null,
        public readonly ?string $input = null,
        public readonly ?bool $validateByRole= null,
        public readonly ?Background $background = null,
        public readonly ?bool $requiresNotification = null
    ){ }
}
```

The code in charge of deciding whether to send the notification or not will have to check the *$requiresNotification* parameter. We will deal with this in the next section.

Creating the Event and the Subscriber

First of all, we need an event to trigger after an operation execution finishes and a subscriber that will keep listening to that event.

```
use Symfony\Contracts\EventDispatcher\Event;

class OperationPerformedEvent extends Event
{
    public function __construct(
```

CHAPTER 3   BACKGROUND EXECUTION OF API OPERATIONS

```php
        public readonly OperationMetadata $operationMetadata,
        public readonly mixed $inputData,
        public readonly mixed $outputData,
        public readonly ?UserInterface $user
    ){}
}
```

The above event carries with it the following data:

- **operationMetadata**: The operation metadata.

- **inputData**: The operation input data from the ApiInput model.

- **outputData**: The operation result data from the ApiOutput model.

- **user**: The operation user. It can be null because not all operations require the user. Only those which implement the OperationRequiresUserInterface.

Now, let's code the subscriber, which will keep listening to the **OperationPerformedEvent** event.

```php
use Symfony\Component\EventDispatcher\EventSubscriberInterface;

class OperationSubscriber implements EventSubscriberInterface
{
    public static function getSubscribedEvents(): array
    {
        return [
            OperationPerformedEvent::class =>
            'onOperationPerformed'
        ];
    }
```

```
    public function onOperationPerformed(OperationPerformedEve
    nt $event): void
    {

    }
}
```

As we have said, the subscriber will keep listening to the **OperationPerformedEvent** event and will execute the **onOperationPerformed** method after the event has been triggered. We will define the method content later.

Creating the Notifier Service

The notifier service should send the notification to the user.

```
class Notifier {

    public function notify(string $operation, mixed $inputData,
    mixed $outputData, ?UserInterface $user) : void
    {

    }
}
```

The notify method is empty. In this method, we would write the necessary code to send the notification. We could send an email using a service like Amazon or an SMS using a service like Twilio. We should inject the notifier service into the subscriber and use it in the **onOperationPerformed** method. The **notify** method receives the operation name, the input and output data, and the user as parameters.

Handling the Notification Based on the Operation

Operations that require sending a notification could manage it differently. That is why we need to encapsulate the notification logic for each operation in different services.

Creating a NotificationHandlerInterface

This interface will define the contract that all notification handlers will have to implement.

```
use Symfony\Component\Security\Core\User\UserInterface;

interface NotificationHandlerInterface {

    public function handleNotification(mixed $inputData, mixed $outputData, ?UserInterface $user);
}
```

The handlers will have to implement the sending notification logic within the *handleNotification* method.

Creating a Notification Handler

Below, we are showing the notification handler for the SendPayment operation. It implements the **NotificationHandlerInterface** defining the *handleNotification* method. Within this method, we would implement the sending logic (SMS, email ...). As required by the interface, the **handleNotification** method receives the input and output data and the user. The user can be null since not all operations require it.

It is important to take into account that most notifications will need the user since the notification is normally send to the user.

```
use App\Api\Notification\NotificationHandlerInterface;
use Symfony\Component\Security\Core\User\UserInterface;
```

```php
class SendPaymentNotificationHandler implements 
NotificationHandlerInterface {

    public function handleNotification(mixed $inputData, mixed 
    $outputData, ?UserInterface $user) : void
    {
    
    }
}
```

But, how can we link handlers with operations? Let's rely on Symfony Service Subscribers to achieve that goal.

Creating the Service Subscriber

Service Subscribers give us access to a set of predefined services while instantiating them only when needed through a Service Locator, a separated lazy-loaded container. Let's write the service subscriber.

```php
use App\Api\Notification\Types\SendPaymentNotificationHandler;
use App\Security\Miscelanea\OperationNames;
use Psr\Container\ContainerInterface;
use Symfony\Contracts\Service\ServiceSubscriberInterface;

class NotificationHandlerSubscriber implements 
ServiceSubscriberInterface
{
    public function __construct(
        private readonly ContainerInterface $locator,
    ) { }

    public static function getSubscribedServices(): array
    {
        return [
            OperationNames::SendPayment->name => SendPaymentNotificationHandler::class
```

        ];
    }
    public function getHandler(string $operationName):
    NotificationHandlerInterface
    {
        return $this->locator->get($operationName);
    }
}

The service subscriber is pretty straightforward. The constructor injects the locator, which will only hold the services defined in the **getSubscribedServices** method. The **getSubscribedServices** method loads the available services with a key-value array, on which the keys are the service key (we use operation names as keys) and the value is the service class. The **getHandler** method uses the locator service to return the service related to the *$operationName* argument.

Using the Service Subscriber

Finally, we must use the subscriber to send the notification using the right handler. Let's modify the **Notifier** service.

```
use Symfony\Component\Security\Core\User\UserInterface;

class Notifier {

    public function __construct(
        private readonly NotificationHandlerSubscriber
        $notificationHandlerSubscriber
    ){}

    public function notify(string $operation, mixed $inputData,
    mixed $outputData, ?UserInterface $user) : void
    {
```

```
            $handler = $this->notificationHandlerSubscriber->
            getHandler($operation);
            $handler->handleNotification($inputData,
            $outputData, $user);
        }
    }
```

Now, the **Notifier** service uses the corresponding handler according to the operation name. It injects the recently created **NotificationHandlerSubscriber** and uses it to get the handler. Then, it uses the handler to send the notification.

Using the Notifier Service

Having the Notifier service ready, we can use it in the OperationSubscriber.

```
use App\EventSubscriber\Event\OperationPerformedEvent;
use Symfony\Component\EventDispatcher\EventSubscriberInterface;

class OperationSubscriber implements EventSubscriberInterface
{
    public function __construct(
        private readonly Notifier $notifier
    ){}

    public static function getSubscribedEvents(): array
    {
        return [
            OperationPerformedEvent::class =>
            'onOperationPerformed'
        ];
    }

    public function onOperationPerformed(OperationPerformedEvent
    $event): void
```

```
    {
        if($event->operationMetadata->requiresNotification){
            $this->notifier->notify($event->operationMetadata->
            name, $event->inputData, $event->outputData,
            $event->user);
        }
    }
}
```

The **onOperationPerformed** method will only send the notification if the operation requires doing it. It figures out it by checking the metadata **requiresNotification** parameter.

Triggering the Event

So far, we have created the subscriber and created a service where we will place the code to send the notification. Now we have to trigger the event after a backgrounded operation finishes. We will place this code in the OperationMessageHandler.

```
use App\Api\Collection\OperationCollection;
use App\Api\Operation\OperationRequiresUserInterface;
use App\EventSubscriber\Event\OperationPerformedEvent;
use Symfony\Component\EventDispatcher\EventDispatcherInterface;
use Symfony\Component\Messenger\Attribute\AsMessageHandler;

#[AsMessageHandler]
class OperationMessageHandler
{
 public function __construct(
 private readonly OperationCollection $operationCollection,
 private readonly EventDispatcherInterface $eventDispatcher,
 private readonly EntityManagerInterface $em
    ){ }
```

```
    public function __invoke(OperationMessage $message): void
{
    $apiOperation = $this->operationCollection->
    getOperation($message->operation);
    $user = null;
    if($message->user && $apiOperation->handler
    instanceof OperationRequiresUserInterface) {
        $user = $this->em->getRepository(User::class)->find
        OneByEmail($message->user);
        $apiOperation->handler->setUser($user);
    }

    $apiOutput = $apiOperation->handler->perform($message->
    operationInput);
    $this->eventDispatcher->dispatch(
        new OperationPerformedEvent($apiOperation->metadata,
        $message->operationInput, $apiOutput->data, $user),
    );
  }
}
```

We have injected the Symfony event dispatcher service and, after getting the operation result, we use the **dispatch** method to trigger the event. After triggered, the OperationSubscriber will detect the fired event and will react to it. We have also initialized the user with the null value to avoid a "non-defined variable" error when passing it to the event constructor.

Conclusion

To finish this chapter, we have learned how to dispatch an event after a background operation finishes so that we can notify the user. In the next chapter, we will implement the necessary mechanisms so that an endpoint can only execute operations related to its context.

CHAPTER 4

Context-Specific Operations

Throughout the previous chapters, we have learned the following:

- How to create an endpoint that is capable of processing operations based on the request payload content
- How to secure our endpoint and operations
- How to execute operations in the background

In this chapter, we will delve into the process of encapsulating an endpoint within a specific context, ensuring that it can only execute the operations defined for that context. This approach not only enhances the security and clarity of our API but also facilitates the management of multiple controllers by promoting a clear separation of concerns. By doing so, we can streamline our codebase, making it easier to maintain and extend as our application evolves.

It is essential to clarify that we should not conflate the protection of operations, which ensures that only specific roles can execute them, as discussed in Chapter 2, with the concept of contextualizing endpoints. Role-based access control is primarily concerned with user permissions, while contextualization limits the operations available to an endpoint based on its designated context. This distinction promotes a more organized and maintainable code structure. Both strategies can be effectively combined to enhance security. For example, a "Payment" context could permit only payment-related operations, with certain operations restricted to specific roles, thereby ensuring that sensitive actions are performed only by authorized users.

Section 1. Contextualizing an Endpoint

In this section, we are going to build the necessary elements to be able to wrap a endpoint with a context.

The Context Enumeration

To start, we are going to create an enumeration for holding the contexts and the operations related to those contexts.

```
enum Context
{
    case inventoryManagement;
    case payment;
    case orderManagement;

    public function getAllowedOperations()
    {
        match($this) {
            self::inventoryManagement => [
                'AddInventoryItem',
                'UpdateInventoryItem',
                'RemoveInventoryItem',
                'ListInventoryItems'
            ],
            self::payment => [
                'SendPayment',
```

CHAPTER 4   CONTEXT-SPECIFIC OPERATIONS

```
            'RefundPayment',
            'ChargePayment'
        ],
        self::orderManagement => [
            'CreateOrder',
            'UpdateOrder',
            'CancelOrder'
        ]
    };
  }
}
```

The above enumeration contains the following cases:

- **inventoryManagement**: Represents the context for the inventory management-related operations.

- **payment**: Represents the context for the payment-related operations.

- **orderManagement**: Represents the context for the order management operations.

The **getAllowedOperations** method returns an array holding the context-allowed operations.

The OperationContext Attribute

In this section, we are going to create the attribute by which we will wrap an endpoint with a context.

```
use App\Api\Context;

#[\Attribute(\Attribute::TARGET_METHOD)]
class OperationContext
```

```
{
    public function __construct(
        public readonly Context $context
    ){ }
}
```

As you can see, the **OperationContext** attribute constructor receives a *Context* enumeration as a parameter. This allows us to simply specify the context, as we are going to see in the next section.

Wrapping an Endpoint with a Context

In this section, we are going to use the **OperationContext** attribute to specify the operation-oriented endpoint context.

```
#[Route('/inventory-management/operation', name: 'api_inventory_management_operation', methods: ['POST'])]
#[OperationContext(Context::inventoryManagement)]
public function inventoryManagementOperationsAction(#[MapRequestPayload] ApiInput $apiInput): JsonResponse
{
    $apiOutput = $this->apiOperationHandler->performOperation($apiInput);
    return new JsonResponse($apiOutput->data, $apiOutput->code);
}

#[Route('/payment/operation', name: 'api_payment_operation', methods: ['POST'])]
#[OperationContext(Context::payment)]
public function paymentOperationsAction(#[MapRequestPayload] ApiInput $apiInput): JsonResponse
{
```

```
    $apiOutput = $this->apiOperationHandler->
    performOperation($apiInput);
      return new JsonResponse($apiOutput->data, $apiOutput->code);
}
#[Route('/order-management/operation', name: 'api_order_
management_operation', methods: ['POST'])]
#[OperationContext(Context::orderManagement)]
  public function orderManagementOperationsAction(#[MapRequest
  Payload] ApiInput $apiInput): JsonResponse
{
    $apiOutput = $this->apiOperationHandler->
    performOperation($apiInput);
      return new JsonResponse($apiOutput->data,
      $apiOutput->code);
}
```

As you can see, we have used the **OperationContext** attribute to specify that each endpoint can only execute its context-allowed operations.

Conclusion

In this section, we have created a PHP enumeration that centralizes the allowable operations for a specific context, and we have implemented an **OperationContext** attribute to specify the operations that can be executed within a controller. Finally, we have created three different endpoints (one for each context) and we have wrapped them with the **OperationContext** attribute passing to its constructor the corresponding context.

In the next section, we will create a dedicated subscriber to listen to the Symfony KernelController event. The subscriber will have to determine whether the requested operation execution can be performed by the endpoint.

Section 2. Detecting Endpoints in a Context Specified

We need a way to detect that a request has been routed to a context-specified endpoint so that we can check if the operation to execute is allowed. To achieve this, let's rely on the Symfony controller kernel event.

Listening to the Kernel Controller Event

We are going to add a method in the KernelSubscriber class that we created in Chapter 1 to listen to the controller event.

An Exception for Informing About Context Invalid Operations

Before coding the event-associated subscriber, let's write the exception that will be thrown when the operation cannot be performed.

```
use Symfony\Component\HttpKernel\Attribute\WithHttpStatus;

#[WithHttpStatus(403)]
class InvalidContextForOperationException extends
\RuntimeException
{
    public function __construct(string $context, string
    $operation, int $code = 403, ?\Throwable $previous = null)
    {
        $msg = sprintf('Operation %s does not belong to context
        %s', $operation, $context);
        parent::__construct($msg, $code, $previous);
    }
}
```

The above exception extends the PHP **RuntimeException**. The "**WithHttpStatus**" attribute is responsible for the HTTP response that will be sent to the client when the exception is thrown, while the "$code" variable refers to the error code of the exception itself. In this specific case, both are set to 403, but they could be different if desired. We use a 403 Access Denied exception because we are denying access to the execution of an operation, although for different reasons than when we did it in Chapter 3 when we used the Symfony voters.

The Kernel-Controller Subscriber

Now that we have an exception to report context errors, let's finally code the kernel-controller subscriber.

```
public function onKernelController(ControllerEvent $event): void
{
    $controllerAttributes = $event->getAttributes();

    $operationContextAttributes = $controllerAttributes[Operation
    Context::class] ?? null;

if(count($operationContextAttributes) > 0) {
$operationContextAttribute = $operationContextAttributes[0];
$apiInput = $this->validationHandler->
deserializeAndValidate($event->getRequest()->getContent(),
ApiInput::class, null);
if(!in_array($apiInput->operation, $operationContextAttribute->
context->getAllowedOperations())) {
throw new InvalidContextForOperationException($operationContext
Attribute->context->name, $apiInput->operation);
}
}
}
```

The above listener works as follows:

- It checks whether the event-associated controller is annotated with the OperationContext attribute.

- If the controller is wrapped with that attribute, it checks whether the operation can be executed using the *getAllowedOperations* method of the Context enum. If do not, it throws an InvalidContextForOperationException to inform about the error.

Checking for an InvalidContextForOperationException in the KernelSubscriber

As we have done with all exceptions so far, we must instruct the **KernelSubscriber** subscriber so that it can detect this exception and format the message as JSON.

```
if($exception instanceof InvalidContextForOperationException){
    $event->setResponse(new JsonResponse([
        'errors' => [
            'operation_endpoint_context' => $exception->
            getMessage()
        ]
    ], 400));
}
```

As you can see, we have only been added another condition for the **InvalidContextForOperationException**.

Conclusion

Again, we have resorted to Symfony's event system to capture the controller requests. This way, we can check whether the controller method is decorated with the OperationContext attribute and, if so, ensure that the context allows the requested operation execution.

In the next chapter, we will create the necessary application tests to ensure that our API behaves as expected.

CHAPTER 5

Testing the API

Having constructed and secured our operation-oriented API, it's crucial to solidify its functionality and ensure it behaves as intended. This final chapter will show you how to use Symfony application tests to check the API works as expected.

Section 1. Creating the Test Class

The Symfony Test Pack component allows us to easily create a test class by using the Symfony maker, so let's use it to automatically generate the test class.

```
bin/console make:test
```

After executing the above command, it will require you to enter some input to create the test class:

- **The test type you want to generate**: Choose the *WebTestCase* type.
- **The name of the class**: Write the name you want.

After it is finished, it will generate the test class in the */tests/* directory at the root of the project typically as *tests/Controller/ApiControllerTest.php*. If we open the test class, we will see something like this:

```
namespace App\Tests;

use Symfony\Bundle\FrameworkBundle\Test\WebTestCase;
```

```
class ApiControllerTest extends WebTestCase
{
    public function testSomething(): void
    {
        $client = static::createClient();
        $crawler = $client->request('GET', '/');

        $this->assertResponseIsSuccessful();
        $this->assertSelectorTextContains('h1', 'Hello World');
    }
}
```

The class contains an example test (*testSomething*). Let's examine its content line by line:

1. Creates a client instance so we can make requests
2. Executes a GET request to the URL
3. Checks that the response status code is in the 200–299 range
4. Checks whether the h1 selector contains the "Hello World" text

This is only a template. If you run the test as is, it will fail because the "/" route and the expected HTML content (<h1>Hello World</h1>) do not exist in the application yet.

Let's write our tests in the next section.

Conclusion

In this section, we explored how to create a test class using the Symfony Test Pack component with the help of the Symfony maker. By executing the command *bin/console make:test*, we can easily generate a template for our test class, which includes a basic example test. In the next section, we are going to fill the test class with a set of tests so that we can cover the maximum number of use cases possible.

Section 2. The API Tests

The following sections show a bunch of tests which test a specific case of use.

> To be able to send our custom HTTP headers, specifically the authentication token, we must prefix the header keys with the "HTTP_" string.

When creating your own tests, you should use your User fixtures authentication tokens to authenticate against the API.

Test a Successful Operation Execution

This test checks that an operation is performed successfully.

```php
public function testOperationSuccess(): void
{
    $client = static::createClient();
    $client->request('POST', '/api/v1/operation', [], [], [
        'HTTP_X-AUTH-TOKEN' => 'fYDg7nMhlvxAtL7KfBnS',
        'HTTP_Content-Type' => 'application/json'
    ], json_encode([
        'operation' => 'SendPayment',
        'data' => [
            'amount' => 13.69,
            'receiver' => 'hghgfyyfg'
        ]
    ]));

    $this->assertResponseStatusCodeSame(200);
}
```

The test sends an existing token, the operation payload contains an existing operation, and the required parameters are valid so that the test should return a *200 HTTP OK* code.

Test a Successful Background Operation

This test checks that an operation is successfully sent to the background. For this test, you will have to create an operation in which metadata attribute sets the operation as background. In Chapter 3, we learned how to achieve that by passing a Background class instance to the "background" parameter of the **OperationMetadata** attribute.

```php
public function testBackgroundOperation(): void
{
    $client = static::createClient();
    $client->request('POST', '/api/v1/operation', [], [], [
        'HTTP_X-AUTH-TOKEN' => 'fYDg7nMhlvxAtL7KfBnS',
        'HTTP_Content-Type' => 'application/json'
    ], json_encode([
        'operation' => 'SendPaymentBackground',
        'data' => [
            'amount' => 13.69,
            'receiver' => 'hghgfyyfg'
        ]
    ]));

    $this->assertResponseStatusCodeSame(202);
}
```

As the operation is flagged as background, the test should return a *202 ACCEPTED* code.

Test Invalid Operation Data

In this case, we are going to test that an operation cannot be performed because the sent data is invalid.

```php
public function testOperationInvalidData(): void
{
    $client = static::createClient();
    $client->request('POST', '/api/v1/operation', [], [], [
        'HTTP_X-AUTH-TOKEN' => 'fYDg7nMhlvxAtL7KfBnS',
        'HTTP_Content-Type' => 'application/json'
    ], json_encode([
        'operation' => 'SendPayment',
        'data' => [
            'amount' => 0,
            'receiver' => 'hghgfyyfg'
        ]
    ]));

    $this->assertResponseStatusCodeSame(400);
}
```

The test sends an invalid payload since the amount parameter must be greater than 0. It should return a *400 Bad request* response. This test assumes that the operation input model contains an amount parameter, and such a parameter is wrapped by a Symfony **GreaterThan** validation constraint which specifies that the amount value must be greater than 0. Let's remember how the input model created in the first chapter looked like.

```php
readonly class SendPaymentInput
{
    public function __construct(
        #[Assert\NotBlank(message: 'Receiver cannot be empty')]
```

CHAPTER 5 TESTING THE API

```
        public string $receiver,
        #[Assert\NotBlank(message: 'Amount cannot be empty')]
        #[Assert\GreaterThan(0, message: 'Amount must be
        greater than 0')]
        public floatlint $amount,
        public ?string $label = null
    ){}
}
```

As you can see above, the amount parameter cannot be empty nor 0.

Test an Unexisting Operation

This test checks that an operation cannot be performed since it does not exist.

```
public function testUnexistingOperation(): void
{
    $client = static::createClient();
    $client->request('POST', '/api/v1/operation', [], [], [
        'HTTP_X-AUTH-TOKEN' => 'fYDg7nMhlvxAtL7KfBnS',
        'HTTP_Content-Type' => 'application/json'
    ], json_encode([
        'operation' => 'SendPayme',
        'data' => [
            'amount' => 0,
            'receiver' => 'hghgfyyfg'
        ]
    ]));

    $this->assertResponseStatusCodeSame(404);
}
```

The test sends an invalid operation name so that a *404 Not Found* response code should be returned.

Test Missing Operation

The test checks that an operation request validation fails since the operation name has not been sent.

```
public function testMissingOperationName(): void
{
    $client = static::createClient();
    $client->request('POST', '/api/v1/operation', [], [], [
        'HTTP_X-AUTH-TOKEN' => 'zPLhK8iQqg9fg7u5jnp',
        'HTTP_Content-Type' => 'application/json'
    ], json_encode([
        'operation' => '',
        'data' => [
            'amount' => 13.69,
            'receiver' => 'hghgfyyfg'
        ]
    ]));

    $this->assertResponseStatusCodeSame(422);
}
```

The test sends a valid data payload; however, the operation name is missing, which should result in a *422 UnprocessableEntityHttpException* code being returned. This response occurs because the absence of the operation name triggers an exception during the validation of the **ApiInput** model. Specifically, this happens when the request reaches the controller, where the Symfony **MapRequestPayload** attribute performs the validation and subsequently throws the *UnprocessableEntityHttpException*.

CHAPTER 5   TESTING THE API

Test an Invalid User Token

This test checks that an operation is not performed because the token sent is invalid

```php
public function testInvalidAuth(): void
{
    $client = static::createClient();
    $client->request('POST', '/api/v1/operation', [], [], [
        'HTTP_X-AUTH-TOKEN' => 'fYDg7AtL7KfBnS',
        'HTTP_Content-Type' => 'application/json'
    ], json_encode([
        'operation' => 'SendPayment',
        'data' => [
            'amount' => 13.69,
            'receiver' => 'hghgfyyfg'
        ]
    ]));

    $this->assertResponseStatusCodeSame(401);
}
```

The test sends the right payload, but the header "X-AUTH-TOKEN" contains an invalid token, so the response code should be *401 Unauthorized*.

Testing Unauthorized User

This test checks that, as the user does not have the right role, the API rejects the operation execution.

```php
public function testUnauthorizedToExecuteOperation(): void
{
    $client = static::createClient();
    $client->request('POST', '/api/v1/operation', [], [], [
```

```
        'HTTP_X-AUTH-TOKEN' => 'vWvn1GOu2Lx5foFgQrRp',
        'HTTP_Content-Type' => 'application/json'
    ], json_encode([
        'operation' => 'SendPayment',
        'data' => [
            'amount' => 13.69,
            'receiver' => 'hghgfyyfg'
        ]
    ]));

    $this->assertResponseStatusCodeSame(403);
}
```

The test sends the right payload and an existing user token, but this user does not hold the right role, so the returned code should be *403 Forbidden*. For executing this test, we should create a user holding a role that is not allowed to execute the **SendPayment** operation and use its token for the test.

Testing an Invalid Context

This test tries to request an operation execution which is not allowed for the context.

```
public function testInvalidContext(): void
{
    $client = static::createClient();
    $client->request('POST', '/api/v1/inventory-management/operation', [], [], [
        'HTTP_X-AUTH-TOKEN' => 'fYDg7nMhlvxAtL7KfBnS',
        'HTTP_Content-Type' => 'application/json'
    ], json_encode([
        'operation' => 'SendPayment',
```

```
        'data' => [
            'amount' => 13.69,
            'receiver' => 'hghgfyyfg'
        ]
    ]));

    $this->assertResponseStatusCodeSame(403);
}
```

The test sends the right payload and a valid user token, but as the *SendPayment* operation cannot be executed in the *inventory-management* context, a *403 Forbidden* response code should be returned.

Making a Short Refactory

You should notice that all the tests share the same code to send the API request. To improve readability and avoid duplication, we can create a private method to perform the API request.

```
private function postOperation(array $payload, string $token,
string $uri = '/api/v1/operation'): void
{
static::createClient()->request('POST', $uri, [], [], [
'HTTP_X-AUTH-TOKEN' => $token,
'HTTP_Content-Type' => 'application/json',
], json_encode($payload));
}
```

The above method receives the payload to send, the authentication token, and the URI to call. The URI parameter holds the "/api/v1/operation" path as a default value because it is used in most tests.

Then we can use this method in our tests. For instance, let's use it in the invalid context test.

```
public function testInvalidContext(): void
{
    $this->postOperation([
        'operation' => 'SendPayment',
        'data' => [
            'amount' => 13.69,
            'receiver' => 'hghgfyyfg'
        ]], 'vWvn1GOu2Lx5foFgQrRp');

    $this->assertResponseStatusCodeSame(403);
}
```

As you can see, thanks to this change, we stop repeating the logic of sending the request. We only need the payload and the authentication token in each test.

Executing the Tests

To execute the test, we have to execute the following command from the project root folder:

```
bin/phpunit
```

This will execute all your tests.

Conclusion

This chapter has provided a detailed guide on how to implement effective tests for an API using Symfony. Through various examples, we have learned to verify the expected behavior of operations, from successful execution to error handling and validations. These tests not only ensure the functionality of the API but also help maintain code quality throughout development. By integrating these testing practices, developers can ensure that their API is robust and reliable, thereby enhancing the overall experience for end users.

Afterword

Throughout this journey, we have explored the intricacies of crafting powerful and versatile operation-oriented APIs using PHP and the Symfony framework. We have traversed the path from defining operations and their input/output models to implementing security measures and optimizing performance with background execution. This afterword serves as a final reflection on the key takeaways and the advantages that an operation-oriented approach offers in the realm of API development.

Key Takeaways

- **Structured Approach**: Promote well-defined operations encapsulated within individual services, fostering modularity and maintainability.
- **Flexibility**: New operations can be seamlessly integrated without disrupting existing ones, ensuring your API can evolve alongside your application.
- **Security**: By leveraging Symfony's security features, we have established a multi-layered approach to securing the API. This includes authentication to ensure only authorized users can perform operations and authorization mechanisms using voters to further restrict or grant access based on specific user roles or conditions.

AFTERWORD

- **Performance Optimization**: Background execution with Symfony Messenger allows us to handle non-critical operations asynchronously, keeping the API responsive even under heavy load.

Benefits

- **Enhanced Maintainability**: Promote code organization and reusability, making maintenance and future modifications significantly easier.

- **Scalability**: The modular design allows for smooth scaling as the API requirements grow, enabling us to add new operations efficiently.

- **Improved Developer Experience**: The clear separation of concerns promotes a well-structured codebase, fostering a more enjoyable and productive development experience.

Disadvantages

- **Learning Curve**: For teams unfamiliar with the operation-oriented paradigm, there may be a steep learning curve. Understanding how to effectively design and implement operations, as well as manage their interactions, can require additional training and experience.

- **Potential for Redundancy**: As new operations are added, there is a risk of redundancy if similar functionalities are implemented across different services. This can lead to code duplication and increased maintenance efforts. Here, if many operations share some logic, it would be key to extract it to other services.

Real-World Applications

Beyond theoretical advantages, the operation-oriented approach would excel in various practical scenarios. Here are some examples:

- **E-commerce Platforms**: User actions like adding items to carts, processing payments, and managing orders can be implemented as distinct operations within an operation-oriented API. This facilitates the addition of new features like loyalty programs or subscription services without compromising existing functionalities.

- **Social Media Applications**: Building APIs for interacting with social media platforms can benefit greatly from an operation-oriented approach. Each action, such as following users or liking comments, can be defined as a dedicated operation. This structure ensures a scalable and maintainable API, allowing for seamless integration of new features like group chats or live video streaming.

- **IoT (Internet of Things) Applications**: Building APIs for interacting with various IoT devices often involves handling diverse data streams and functionalities. An operation-oriented approach provides a solid structure for defining operations related to device control, data retrieval, and configuration management, leading to a robust and maintainable API.

AFTERWORD

Conclusion

By adopting an operation-oriented approach, we can equip our APIs with the power to handle complex functionalities in a structured, secure, and performant manner. This approach empowers you to build APIs that adapt to evolving business needs, ensuring their longevity and resilience within your application ecosystem.

GPSR Compliance

The European Union's (EU) General Product Safety Regulation (GPSR) is a set of rules that requires consumer products to be safe and our obligations to ensure this.

If you have any concerns about our products, you can contact us on

ProductSafety@springernature.com

In case Publisher is established outside the EU, the EU authorized representative is:

Springer Nature Customer Service Center GmbH
Europaplatz 3
69115 Heidelberg, Germany

www.ingramcontent.com/pod-product-compliance
Lightning Source LLC
LaVergne TN
LVHW021958060526
838201LV00048B/1617